GOD IS SPEAKING TO YOU

100 Devotions to Hear His Voice

ADRIAN GHIDUC

God Is Speaking to You
100 Devotions to Hear His Voice
by Adrian Guiduc
Copyright © 2021

Interior Text Formatting: affordablechristianediting.com
Cover Design: Jeff Zdrentan

ISBN 978-1-7356426-9-7 (Paperback)
ISBN 978-1-7356426-3-5 (HC)
ISBN 978-1-7356426-0-4 (eBook)

Printed and Bound in the United States

Dedication

To my precious son, Edwin Jensen,
who went to heaven too soon.

TABLE OF CONTENTS

My heart has heard you say,
"Come and talk with me."
And my heart responds,
"LORD, I am coming."

– Psalm 27:8

1

STEP FORTH WITH CONFIDENCE

Have I not commanded you? Be strong and courageous.
Do not be afraid; do not be discouraged, for the LORD
your God will be with you wherever you go. – Joshua 1:9

The road before you is new. You must conquer this land and walk through it with confidence, knowing that the Lord is on your side. You have not yet conquered all of the lands that He has destined to belong to you. Every step you take alongside of Him will build confidence in your life.

Joshua stood before millions of people whom God had commissioned him to lead to the Promised Land. This land to be conquered was a yet unknown territory, like a dark forest the people had to enter. The entire populace was gazing at Joshua to ascertain the attitude he projected toward the unknown. Fear or courage? The leader's attitude was transmitted through the ranks of people who read his attitude more than anything else. The presence of the Lord was the place where Joshua drew the sap of his courage. The Lord's words to Joshua built his confidence and courage within to advance into the unknown in life.

Each day, you also stand before an unknown land. This territory holds His trials and challenges. You will cross it daringly if you draw the sap of your courage from the presence of the

Lord. The only way to move ahead daringly and with courage is to constantly listen to His assurances for your life. The more you stay in His presence, the more courage, confidence and power will develop in your life. You will advance with assurance because He will smooth the road beneath your feet. Those closest to you need you to pass courage to them through your attitude; this is the fuel you receive when you stay in His presence.

When you draw your sap from My presence, the fibers of confidence and courage will develop in your heart. You will advance through the day that you are facing, daring, like a young lion, certain that I am your shadow on your right hand. I will always walk beside you and support you. Listen to My voice and My plans, and you will be able to advance despite your inadequacies. I am on your side and, at the right time, I will reveal the necessary resources that I have prepared for you.

"Be strong and courageous. Do not be afraid or terrified because of them, for the LORD your God goes with you; he will never leave you nor forsake you."
– Deuteronomy 31:6

"For the LORD your God is the one who goes with you to fight for you against your enemies to give you victory."
– Deuteronomy 20:4

2

I GIVE YOU MY PEACE

Peace I leave with you; my peace I give you. I do not give to you as the world gives. Do not let your hearts be troubled and do not be afraid. – John 14:27

The world is troubled around you, but the Lord wants to instill an atmosphere of peace in your mind—one that surpasses any understanding. His rays of peace will flood the dark room and the curtains of worry from your soul and light it with His presence, His promises, and hope. The more you stand before God, the more the rays of His presence will chase away the shadows of fear; joy will invade your soul and mind.

Many people feel stressed and sorrowful; others are paralyzed from fear. In fact, that is how the disciples were in the upstairs room after the Lord's resurrection. They hid, but the Lord came into the chamber filled with followers full of fear, and His presence shattered the heavy atmosphere. He brought them His peace that surpasses all understanding.

Perhaps in the chamber of your soul, the shadows of fear have appeared and are projecting strange shadows on the walls of your soul. When you allow God to get in with His reflector light of the Word and the Holy Spirit, any shadows will disappear. His presence, which shines like gold, makes doubt disappear and embeds courage and bravery.

I want to give you My peace, which transcends all understanding. I want My peace to descend upon your mind and into your soul as they are shadowed by the fear of the unknown and chase away any shadow brought by the Evil One. I am with you; I am on your side and want to support you. The God of the universe is on your side. Speak to me about your sorrows, and My Spirit will comfort and will guide you. My Presence will be strong like the sun in all its splendor, and any shadow of doubt will be chased away.

On the evening of that first day of the week when the disciples were together with the doors locked for fear of the Jewish leaders, Jesus came. As He stood among them, He said with simple directness, "Peace be with you!" Jesus repeated again, "Peace be with you! As the Father has sent me, I am sending you."
– John 20:19, 21

And the peace of God, which transcends all understanding, will guard your hearts and your minds in Christ Jesus. – Philippians 4:7

*For the L*ORD *God is a sun and shield; the L*ORD *bestows favor and honor; no good thing does he withhold from those whose walk is blameless.*
– Psalm 84:11

3

GUIDANCE

The LORD will guide you always; he will satisfy your needs in a sun-scorched land and will strengthen your frame. You will be like a well-watered garden, like a spring whose waters never fail. – Isaiah 58:11

Guidance doesn't mean that you will know the Lord's whole plan from the beginning. He will not show you the map from the beginning, but He will help you take each step to reach your destination. Over the course of life's journey, you need faith and a close connection with God in order to avoid getting sidetracked.

When you let yourself be guided by God, you won't know all of the details of the journey He has planned for you. When your loved ones ask you for mathematical and logical explanations about the final aim, you will often not know how to answer them. Your loved ones will judge you and accuse you but do not doubt His plan. Do not doubt in the darkness what you heard in the light.

When God guided Abraham to the Promised Land, He did not give His servant all of the details of the journey. God did not tell him how the road would be and when he would arrive, but he went based on the Lord's trustworthy character and promises.

When the Lord guides you in a certain direction or to a certain work He wants you to do, neither will He give you all of the elements of the journey. God will reveal step by step what you have to do and staying in close contact with Him reveals a life lived in faith. When you do not rely on your own resources but on the Lord's resources and power, you are living by faith.

Be steadfast in moments of doubt. Keep the message He sent you close to your heart. Sooner or later, the steps that you take guided by Him will prove to be best.

I don't make mistakes in what I do and how I guide. When you spend time with Me, I reveal My plans to you. I will reveal things you haven't seen, which have been hidden from your view. I will tell you how to take steps before certain things happen. Stay in touch with Me permanently. Trust in Me beyond what you can see.

Show me your ways, LORD, teach me your paths. Guide me in your truth and teach me, for you are God my Savior, and my hope is in you all day long.
– Psalm 25:4-5

The LORD had said to Abram, "Go from your country, your people and your father's household to the land I will show you. – Genesis 12:1

Whether you turn to the right or to the left, your ears will hear a voice behind you, saying, "This is the way; walk in it." – Isaiah 30:21

4

THE LORD'S WHISPER

And the Holy Spirit descended on him in bodily form like a dove. And a voice came from heaven: "You are my Son, whom I love; with you I am well pleased. – Luke 3:22

The surrounding world contains background noise, and many shrill voices fight for your attention. These voices want to keep you tied to terrible, shocking news and messages coming in from different parts of the world. But all of this turmoil drowns out the Lord's still, small voice, making it even quieter and less likely to be heard. His voice knocks gently at your mind's door, but you have to maintain a quietness to hear it.

The Holy Spirit descended upon Jesus in the form of a dove to transmit His message because hearing His subdued and soothing voice requires stillness. When you quiet your mind's chamber, the voice of God begins to be heard. He doesn't yell, but rather whispers. He connects the words of the Scripture with the circumstances you are experiencing to give you a solution or encouragement. His voice is gentle like the summer sea breeze, whispering tenderly, "You are My beloved. I am beside you."

Is your ear keen enough to hear His loving whisper? The more time you spend in His presence, the easier it will be to hear Him, and you will see the difference between the voices competing for your attention.

I want to speak to you and advise you. In order to hear My voice, you must have quietness in your life. My voice is tender and calm. The more you spend time in My presence and be attentive, the more you will become accustomed to My voice. Then you will easily be able to hear my whisper in the midst of the turmoil around you. I want to speak to you even in life's bustling moments so you can make the best decisions. I love you with an eternal love, and I will support you in what you have to do on this day. Step forward with immeasurable courage.

Rather, it should be that of your inner self, the unfading beauty of a gentle and quiet spirit, which is of great worth in God's sight. – 1 Peter 3:4

After the earthquake came a fire, but the LORD was not in the fire. And after the fire came a gentle whisper. When Elijah heard it, he pulled his cloak over his face and went out and stood at the mouth of the cave. Then a voice said to him, "What are you doing here, Elijah?"
– 1 Kings 19:12-13

Come to me, all you who are weary and burdened, and I will give you rest. Take my yoke upon you and learn from me, for I am gentle and humble in heart, and you will find rest for your souls.
– Matthew 11:28-29

5

THE CONNECTOR

Now the Syrians on one of their raids had carried off a little girl from the land of Israel, and she worked in the service of Naaman's wife. She said to her mistress, "Would that my LORD were with the prophet who is in Samaria! He would cure him of his leprosy." – 2 Kings 5:2-3 (ESV)

Naaman, a Syrian general who had won many battles for his king, was respected throughout the entire country. After one of the battles, he brought his wife a young Hebrew girl as a helper. The name of this servant girl is unknown, but this nameless girl performed a great service. Even though General Naaman was greatly appreciated and respected, he hid a profound pain beneath his clothes—the incurable disease of leprosy. The pain and suffering from his disease severely impacted the general's life. The little servant girl connected her master's pain in her mind with the healing that God could provide through the prophet Elisha. God used Naaman's maid as the connector who spoke to the suffering man about the healing that only He can bring. Her concern was a step that brought Naaman to healing.

Your role in this world is to connect those with whom you cross paths and those who are suffering with God's power. In the spiritual sense, the connector is the person who links the needy one or the hurting one with resources or the solution that comes only from God.

Perhaps a person you will meet on this day will need your help. Another may need a guiding light, and others will need some encouragement only you can give. Connect those who cross your path with His resources. The words of the connector are like golden apples in a silver basket. The experiences you have had alongside God and that you will tell about will develop the wings of faith of those around you and will help them rise above the storms of sorrow.

Along your road, you will meet people when you least expect who need Me. Some will need an uplifting word, and others will need you to speak to them about My resources or the healing that comes from Me. Be sensitive to what you hear and direct those people's gazes toward Me. I know that, for many around you, life is a marathon with trying to accumulate more and more material possessions. In the end, though, they leave all their belongings behind on earth. Your role is to be My ambassador in this world. I will care for you so that you will have everything necessary but make time to uplift those you meet and those who are fallen.

A word fitly spoken is like apples of gold in a setting of silver. – Proverbs 25:11 (ESV)

Then Peter said, "Silver or gold I do not have, but what I do have I give you. In the name of Jesus Christ of Nazareth, walk." Taking him by the right hand, he helped him up, and instantly the man's feet and ankles became strong. He jumped to his feet and began to walk. Then he went with them into the temple courts, walking and jumping, and praising God.

– Acts 3:6-8

6

Spend Time with Me

She had a sister called Mary, who sat at the Lord's feet listening to what he said. But Martha was distracted by all the preparations that had to be made. She came to him and asked, "Lord, don't you care that my sister has left me to do the work by myself? Tell her to help me!" "Martha, Martha," the Lord answered, "you are worried and upset about many things, but few things are needed--or indeed only one. Mary has chosen what is better, and it will not be taken away from her." – Luke 10:39-42

Quiet time spent in the presence of God will revitalize your life. Just like a glass of cold water revitalizes an overheated man who is tired of working in the sweltering heat of the day, time spent in the presence of God will revitalize your soul. Your thoughts will become clear, and you will know what you really have to do.

This world, which is constantly active, is in a race. Urgent matters call from all sides and having a busy schedule is laudable; however, a trap can result from all this busyness. Life demands more and more from you, and the tendency is to push God aside, or sadly, He ends up in second, third, or fourth place.

Mary and Martha had Jesus as a guest in their house. Martha was caught up with accomplishing so many details that she missed the unique moment to listen to Jesus teaching. Jesus, however, praised Mary because she chose well in prioritizing that special time of sitting at His feet, focusing on what was truly important.

Time spent in the presence of God is unique and guarantees enormous benefits. When you stay in His presence and listen to His voice, the Holy Spirit will make connections between what He says to you and what you must do. The Holy Spirit will guide you in your decisions. Listening to His voice will help resolve the thoughts crowding around your mind's door and revitalize your soul and spirit. Like a freshly sharpened sawblade, your mind will be ready for action. His peace and presence will descend upon you and guide you in an outstanding way. You must resist the tendency to let your crowded schedule shorten or steal the time you share with God.

When you spend time in My presence, I will clear up certain aspects that you do not understand. I will give you peace at the spiritual level to show you in which direction you should go. You will often be caught up in many things that you will have to do, but don't forget that speaking to Me is the most important entry on your schedule. I will give you the wisdom you need to solve problems faster and better. Speak to Me, and I will guide you. Listen to Me, and I will reveal great things that you do not know and will be a great joy for your life.

I will instruct you and teach you in the way you should go; I will counsel you with my loving eye on you.
– Psalm 32:8

One thing I ask from the LORD, this only do I seek: that I may dwell in the house of the LORD all the days of my life, to gaze on the beauty of the LORD and to seek him in his temple. – Psalm 27:4

7

I Light Your Path

Your sun will never set again, and your moon will wane no more; the Lord will be your everlasting light, and your days of sorrow will end. – Isaiah 60:20

Sometimes, the road you will walk along will be well-lit and straight, and it will be easy and beautiful to move along. But other times, you will go through dark valleys not knowing where to step next. In those times, you will need to keep the Lamp—His Word—close to light your path so that you know where to take the next step. The lamp is not a light-house illuminating the way five miles ahead, but a focused light helping you take the next step. God is interested in a relationship of reliance on Him. When you move forward with Him in the dark, your faith will develop, and His voice will become more familiar.

Feeding worry has a way of weaving a dark cloth around you that will envelop you and block the rays of hope from entering your heart. The longer you stay in the light of the reflector of the holy Word, the more the bright rays of His presence will penetrate and dismantle the dark curtain produced by worry.

Sometimes, life's circumstances will bring sorrow, and you will see the night set over you. However, don't forget that those will be the most opportune moments for the Light of the World to shine brightly.

When those around you go through the dark valleys of depression, you must be a ray of hope directing them to He who is the Sun of righteousness.

When you will go through the darkness, I will light up your path. My plan is your reliance on Me. I want you to speak to Me, ask Me, and I will gladly show you and tell you what to do to advance. Each word that I will give you will be a ray of light to help you move forward in My plan. Stay connected to My presence and stay in touch with me. When you see someone stumbling around in the dark, pray for that person and be a ray of hope.

Your word is a lamp for my feet, a light on my path.
– Psalm 119:105

The LORD is my light and my salvation—whom shall I fear? The LORD is the stronghold of my life—of whom shall I be afraid? – Psalm 27:1

You, LORD, are my lamp; the LORD turns my darkness into light. – 2 Samuel 22:29

8

My Agenda, His Agenda

Call to me and I will answer you and tell you great and unsearchable things you do not know. – Jeremiah 33:3

Certain elements will influence you to build dreams and an agenda within for you to follow. These plans might take years from your life, and in the end, the results might be unsatisfactory or insignificant. Perhaps you will often tend to bring these plans before God and pray so that He would bless them and stamp His seal of approval on your project.

However, what God wants from you is to fully rely on Him in all aspects. True reliance on Him does not mean fulfillment of your plans; rather, an acceptance of His plans and allowing Him to animate His will for you in your heart brings His presence. His plans and His will for your life far surpass the boundaries of your understanding. They are unattainable without His intervention and help. If you will be an available instrument for God to play the songs of heaven, of peace, and unwavering faith, you will be impressed at how much you will accomplish with His help.

When He reveals His will and the plans He wants to accomplish, you must stay in constant contact with Him in order to know how to act on them. His revelation is something that surpasses your ability to solve and to think. Pray so that you may understand His plans and His will for you. As you take steps in reliance on Him, you will be amazed and humbled as your faith grows.

What I want from you is to pray for big things. Perhaps right now you don't know what to ask for, but when you will lend your ear to My plans, you will understand the direction in which the Holy Spirit's wind blows. If you only pray to Me to approve your plans, they will be small because they will always be tied to your resources, ability and vision. But if you receive and live My plans, they will be sizeable because you will rely on My ability and resources.

Trust in the LORD with all your heart; do not depend on your own understanding. Seek his will in all you do, and he will show you which path to take.
– Proverbs 3:5-6 (NLT)

Pray that the LORD your God will tell us where we should go and what we should do. – Jeremiah 42:3

Many nations will come and say, "Come, let us go up to the mountain of the LORD, to the temple of the God of Jacob. He will teach us his ways, so that we may walk in his paths." The law will go out from Zion, the word of the LORD from Jerusalem. – Micah 4:2

9

I Will Put You in a Better Place

However, as it is written: "What no eye has seen, what no ear has heard, and what no human mind has conceived"—the things God has prepared for those who love him. – 1 Corinthians 2:9

God will put you in a better place than where you are now—somewhere better than where people can get to you or where you can get through your own powers and effort. Many strive to reach better positions and obtain possessions they have long desired. They analyze circumstances, plans, and do everything they can. Nothing is wrong with that—quite the contrary, wishing for your and your family's wellbeing is good.

Sometimes plans succeed and other times they do not come to fruition. God can do more for you than you can do or than those around you can help you do so that He can lead you and show you His imprint on your life's path. He is a good Father who wants to give you relationships, possessions and positions that are beyond your ability to obtain. Thus, He wants to show you that He loves you and has a wonderful life planned for you. Young Joseph had been unjustly accused and thrown in jail. His future looked bleak. He had no connections or opportunities to assist him. However, despite the obstacles blocking him,

God miraculously opened a door and lifted him up. The prisoner became a prince; he left the prison for a palace. Impressive! He had no connections and no diplomas, but he had God on his side who showed favor toward him.

Perhaps you feel shackled—like your hands are tied, lacking connections and opportunities to rise from where you are. Don't forget: God is on your side. He will lift you up, show you His unconditional love, and reveal His outstanding plan for your life. He wants to propel you to a better place. He has already made preparations for you that you cannot yet even imagine. Don't let your current situation or your concern keep you ensnared in the toils of faithlessness. Wait in faith for Him to intervene for you; thank Him because the time will come when He will put you in a better place.

I want to surprise you with certain blessings and show you that I love you. I have arranged for matters to work in your favor so that I can better position you. You try to do different things in your power, and you end up stressed and discouraged. I want to remind you: I will work in your favor in surprising ways. Speak to Me, listen to My whisper, take steps in faith when the time comes and be open to understanding My plan. Be glad that I am on your side and that I work behind the curtains of your life for you. I have prepared a better place for you in order to show you that I love you.

*Then Pharaoh said to Joseph, "Since God has made all
this known to you, there is no one so discerning and
wise as you. You shall be in charge of my palace, and
all my people are to submit to your orders. Only with
respect to the throne will I be greater than you."
So Pharaoh said to Joseph, "I hereby put you
in charge of the whole land of Egypt."*
– Genesis 41:39-41

*And my God will supply every need of yours according
to his riches in glory in Christ Jesus.*
– Philippians 4:19

10

THE GARDEN OF THE HEART

Above all else, guard your heart, for everything you do flows from it. – Proverbs 4:23

Your heart is like a garden, and God is the Gardener. He likes to walk thought the garden of your heart, planting the seeds of faith and enjoying the flowers and fruit growing there. What is planted on the fertile land of your heart will grow and influence your actions, feelings, and your entire life.

Certainly, others will throw in seeds of negativity, envy and sin into your heart's garden. If you leave them there, you will see them take root and bear hideous fruit. This fruit, in turn, will influence your life, actions, and feelings.

The garden of the heart must be guarded, cleaned of the Evil One's weeds that start to take root. The seeds and delicate seedlings must be watered with much faith and protected so that they may bear plentiful fruit. Your role is to differentiate between the Evil One's seeds and God's seeds. The more you fill your heart with God's will, other negative elements will not have room to take root. Guard your heart above all things!

On this day, plant in the garden of your heart flowers that ennoble you. Plant in the gardens of those around you the seeds of faith to transform their lives and to be a pleasant scent before God.

I am the great Gardener, and I want to walk beside you in the garden of your heart. I will light your way and will show you what you have to take out from your heart and what you have to protect, water and allow to grow.

When you will be weary or down, your life will be a lot more vulnerable to accepting the seeds planted by others in your heat. Guard your heart in those times so that the Evil One's seeds cannot be planted. Constantly do a cleaning of your heart. Walk with Me through the garden of your heart and make that garden a corner of Heaven.

In simple humility, let our gardener, God, landscape you with the Word, making a salvation-garden of your life. – James 1:21 (MSG)

But whose delight is in the law of the LORD, and who meditates on his law day and night. That person is like a tree planted by streams of water, which yields its fruit in season and whose leaf does not wither— whatever they do prospers. – Psalm 1:2-3

My heart has heard you say, "Come and talk with me." And my heart responds, "LORD, I am coming." – Psalm 27:8 (NLT)

11

ENJOY EACH STEP

With praise and thanksgiving, they sang to the LORD:
"He is good; his love toward Israel endures forever." And
all the people gave a great shout of praise to the LORD, be-
cause the foundation of the house of the LORD was laid.
– Ezra 3:11

Joy must be part of each step of progress, not just the end. The human tendency is to work tirelessly and, at the end, after resolving a certain situation or after reaching victory, to experience moments of joy. However, joy and gratitude must be a part of every step of progress, as small as it might be, because God helped you get there.

With difficulty, the Hebrew people managed to rebuild the Temple. After they had laid the foundation, they joyfully took a break and offered praise and thanked God for the help given up to that point. The road to finishing the Temple was long and grueling, but during this break for joy and praise, they felt energized and had the opportunity to proclaim that their help came from Him.

During your life, you will be tempted to work hard and constantly until you accomplish certain projects you have undertaken and then enjoy what you have accomplished. However, at times the plans and projects may become the idols that claim all of your energy and attention, making you forget God, who has helped you thus far. If you will stop to thank Him and praise Him after your small accomplishments, your faith and trust in Him will be consolidated. Your accomplishments will help you see God as your help and support—even in spite of any obstacles. The praise you bring will portray in your mind a great God who is on your side and ready to help you. His wish is that your tasks in life will not become more important than your Father-daughter or Father-son relationship with Him.

Remove your eyes from the transitory things in this life and thank Me for the health I have given you and because I am with you. Let joy take over you. Let your heart be full of gratitude because I am on your side. These moments of praise will give you even more strength. I will help you get ahead in the work you have to do, but you must recognize that your accomplishments come from Me. Rejoice and thank Me because I have supported you thus far.

Rejoice always, pray continually, give thanks in all circumstances; for this is God's will for you in Christ Jesus.
– 1 Thessalonians 5:16-18

Samuel then took a large stone and placed it between the towns of Mizpah and Jeshanah. He named it Ebenezer (which means "the stone of help"), for he said, "Up to this point the LORD has helped us!"
– 1 Samuel 7:12 (NLT)

12

The Impact of Spiritual Experiences

Mark out a straight path for your feet so that those who are weak and lame will not fall but become strong.
– Hebrews 12:13 (NLT)

Life swings like a pendulum between moments of joy and moments of crisis. We all will have to pass through the difficult or almost impossible moments with the help of God's intervention. Other times, we will notice divine marks even in smallest of matters. All of these experiences will remain in the history of our faith and will have an impact on the lives of our loved ones. Those around us will see God's presence in our life, thus leaving an example for them to follow when they experience the hard times.

The Bible shares the story of a family shattered when the father, the pillar of the home, passed away, and the mother was left with two children and unimaginable debts. When the creditors came to take her children and enslave them to pay off the debts, this mother received a solution from the prophet Elisha. The solution meant borrowing vessels from all of the neighbors, closing the door after herself and her children, and pouring the remaining oil from her cruse in them. The command was about multiplying the oil and later selling it to cover the debts and support herself and her sons. The children had a part to fulfill—bringing the vessels and then experiencing the miracle that would mark their spiritual lives as well.

The spiritual encounters that we experience will have an impact on the lives of those around us. The way we behave in a crisis will serve to create a paradigm for moments of crisis that our children or those near us will go through. When God answers our prayer, we need to share the experience with those around us. When we see His protection or healing in an outstanding way, we need to tell others to encourage them.

I will give you outstanding spiritual experiences through which you will feel Me near you. They will be authentic, and you will not have any doubts about them. Thus, you will have the courage to share them with others. Through difficult and uplifting experiences in your life, make your faith living, authentic, and palpable. Teach those near you to go through life's crises along with Me but teach them to seek Me also in life's moments of joy. Be an example for them. Put Me first in everything, and you will be victorious.

Teach them his decrees and instructions and show them the way they are to live and how they are to behave.
– Exodus 18:20

Elisha said, "Go around and ask all your neighbors for empty jars. Don't ask for just a few. Then go inside and shut the door behind you and your sons. Pour oil into all the jars, and as each is filled, put it to one side." She left him and shut the door behind her and her sons.

They brought the jars to her and she kept pouring. When all the jars were full, she said to her son, "Bring me another one." But he replied, "There is not a jar left." Then the oil stopped flowing. She went and told the man of God, and he said, "Go, sell the oil and pay your debts. You and your sons can live on what is left."

– 2 Kings 4:3-7

13

BE STILL IN MY PRESENCE

*Be still, and know that I am God; I will be exalted among
the nations, I will be exalted in the earth.* – Psalm 46:10

When you spend time in the presence of God, joy will fill your heart, and He will show you life's path. Do not rush to leave His presence because the blessings you receive there cannot be found anywhere else.

As minutes, days, and years constantly pass, you are trying to accomplish more and taking advantage of as many things as possible. You may have unknowingly found yourself caught in a trap of doing things your way without receiving divine guidance.

But God, who is the beginning and the end, the Alpha and the Omega, who is beyond time and space, invites you to stop in His presence. Stopping before God is not a waste of time; rather, He welcomes you to this place where He reveals the path you should walk. This place fills your heart with joy and shows you how to be more efficient in what you must accomplish. You often rush and work hard to accomplish a great deal but ceasing work to be in His presence will bring along blessings that only He can give you. Guidance, satisfaction, peace and fulfillment come from that stop you make before the One who is Jehova Jireh—"God who will take care of you."

Stop in My presence, speak to Me and listen to Me in the silence of your soul. I want to teach you and whisper to you how you can take the steps to victory and not to failure. I see beyond what you see, and you understand that I can guide you in what you have to do. I will give you joys and spiritual fulfillment that you have never before experienced. Wait; please don't rush to leave My presence. The more you stay in contact with Me, the more I will reveal your blessings and the road you must walk along.

You make known to me the path of life; you will fill me with joy in your presence, with eternal pleasures at your right hand. – Psalm 16:11

Be still before the LORD and wait patiently for him; do not fret when people succeed in their ways, when they carry out their wicked schemes. – Psalm 37:7

Yes, my soul, find rest in God; my hope comes from him. – Psalm 62:5

14

COURAGE DEVELOPS

Your servant has killed both the lion and the bear; this uncircumcised Philistine will be like one of them, because he has defied the armies of the living God. – 1 Samuel 17:36

Courage develops after experiencing victory with the help of the LORD. Every small victory is like a brick that you lay while building the fortress of courage. When you develop courage and bravery from relying on God's power, He is glorified. However, when you develop your courage by relying only on your own abilities, you risk developing the idol of pride in yourself. In whatever you do, be sure to rely on Him.

David had the courage to face the giant Goliath while the entire army of the country quavered in fear. The day-to-day victories David had already experienced gave him the courage to meet the giant. He had trained with his slingshot until he became an expert marksman. When a lion and a bear sought to raid his flock of sheep for a meal, he fought both animals, killing them. Their pelts adorning his tent were evidence of his victories. Victory after victory built up his courage. When David saw Goliath, he was not fearful because his day-to-day victories had developed great courage within him. He charged the giant and became victorious.

When you face your giants in life, you too will have the

courage to charge because, like David, you have experienced victories with the help of the Lord. When faced with life's challenges, you need not rely on your human nature; instead, rely on God's power, promises and character because He has promised that He will never leave you. People who saw what God did for them in the past will charge at life's giants and take on new territories with confidence.

God wants to give you small victories to build great confidence within you. This confidence must not be in yourself, which is idolatrous, but rather in Him. The more you believe and live His promises, the more you will have the courage to charge when faced with life's challenges.

Go forth on this day trusting that I walk beside you. I have great plans for you and victories I want to grant you, but you must develop your courage every day. This courage accompanied by My power will propel you forward in people's eyes because some victories will only be attained through His power meshed together with the courage you have strengthened over time.

*Be strong and courageous. Do not be afraid or terrified because of them, for the L*ORD *your God goes with you; he will never leave you nor forsake you.*
– Deuteronomy 31:6

For the Spirit God gave us does not make us timid, but gives us power, love and self-discipline.
– 2 Timothy 1:7

Have I not commanded you? Be strong and courageous.
Do not be afraid; do not be discouraged, for the LORD
your God will be with you wherever you go."
– Joshua 1:9

15

FIGHT WITH THE RIGHT WEAPONS

Then Saul dressed David in his own tunic. He put a coat of armor on him and a bronze helmet on his head. David fastened on his sword over the tunic and tried walking around, because he was not used to them. "I cannot go in these," he said to Saul, "because I am not used to them." So, he took them off. – 1 Samuel 17:38-39

Trying to be victorious with inadequate weapons and methods will constitute a disadvantage in your battles. You will always be tempted to use earthly weapons in battles that have a spiritual dimension.

When David wanted to go before the giant Goliath, king Saul dressed him in his personal battle uniform and gave him the use of his own weapons. Young David was not acclimated to these weapons of warfare and knew he would be unable to perform when wearing them. Had he accepted Saul's generous offer to use his accoutrements, he most assuredly would have lost the battle. David took them off, picked up his trusted slingshot—the weapon he had trained to use expertly. Thus, the giant was handily defeated, and the Israelites eagerly faced the Philistines.

You will also have to face battles with life's giants. Even if many of these battles seem normal and to be indicative of the human realm, they also have a real spiritual dimension. Train now using the spiritual weapon that God has placed at your disposal. Do not accept earthly weapons that appear shiny and serviceable but will only cause you to lose the war. Even if God's spiritual weapons are not all that impressive in the eyes of others, they were fashioned by God to bring His children victory. The prayers you raise up will have tremendous power, faith will be a shield to protect you from the Evil One's arrows, and the Word is the sword of the Holy Spirit, which will help you flourish. Use all of the spiritual weapons that God places at your disposal, and you will be able to create a path to victory in any jungle.

I clothe you in power and want you to get ahead in life's battles in My name and depending on Me. Don't forget that you need not engage in all of the battles that appear before you because the Evil One will try to divert you from My plan by keeping you busy with various insignificant battles. Choose your battles carefully. Don't respond to any insults. Speak to Me about them. Choose to fight only in those battles that will help you to fulfill the plan that I have designed for you. I have placed powerful weapons at your disposal to enable you to fight and attain victory. Train with these weapons day after day, and when the time for battle comes, you will be more than victorious.

Therefore, put on the full armor of God, so that when the day of evil comes, you may be able to stand your ground, and after you have done everything, to stand. – Ephesians 6:13

16

I Walk Beside You

Even though I walk through the darkest valley, I will fear no evil, for you are with me; your rod and your staff, they comfort me. – Psalm 23:4

When you go through dark moments, do not doubt what God has promised you in light. The times when you go through deep valleys will give you the impression that they are never-ending. Thus, in your heart, an environment of doubt and uncertainty can easily be created. Those are times when you must look for the presence of God at any cost so that His rays can light up the darkness that has descended upon your soul.

David would say, *"Though I walk through the valley of the shadow of death, I will fear no evil, for You are with me."* In times when you are in valleys, you must never doubt the fact that He is with you and that He will walk beside you step by step through the valley of shadows. His promises still stand in the difficult times in life. Doubting His promises is a form of faithlessness.

You are only passing through the dark valley, and that is not where you should camp out as though it is your permanent residence. During this passing, God will be a flame post that will give you light and show you the way out. He will give you signs to tell you that He is by your side and works in your favor.

When you go through the valley of doubt, you will often feel alone but do not forget that I walk beside you. What I showed you in the light does not change in the darkness. Keep going on your journey; My promises still stand, and I will honor them. My character does not change. You can move forward with the confidence that I am with you, and I will help you cross the area of doubt and the valley of pain. I will help you to climb the mountain of victory. Perhaps you know a loved one who is going through a time of pressure. Tell that person that I am with him or her.

Because of your great compassion you did not abandon them in the wilderness. By day the pillar of cloud did not fail to guide them on their path, nor the pillar of fire by night to shine on the way they were to take.
– Nehemiah 9:19

The Lord is my light and my salvation—so why should I be afraid? The Lord is my fortress, protecting me from danger, so why should I tremble?
– Psalm 27:1 (NLT)

17

Do Not Be Surprised

You will drink from the brook, and I have directed the ravens to supply you with food there." The ravens brought him bread and meat in the morning and bread and meat in the evening, and he drank from the brook.
– 1 Kings 17:4, 6

"Don't be surprised when you see who I use to help My work progress and blessings come over you." Sometimes God wants to amaze you with a lesson that is designed to knock down certain preconceived notions you have created in your mind. Each person has certain preconceived ideas about the way in which God works and those whom He uses. And often, the methods or agents He uses will not coincide with what you imagine or what you expect.

Elijah was hiding at the Brook Cherith during a period of great drought and hunger throughout the entire country. God ordered the ravens to feed him. Who knows? Perhaps the ravens carried pieces of meat and food from the king's table and brought them to Elijah. In that culture, the ravens were considered unclean birds, but God used them as special agents in His plan to feed Elijah.

What God wants from you is for you not to put boundaries on His work and on the tools He will use. He wants to surprise you with new things and people that He uses to help you get ahead and bless you. Beyond the tools, He looks at who He chooses to use, commanding them to act in one way or another. Don't be surprised if He will send His "ravens"—unclean animals—to come help you. Let God go beyond the boundaries of your understanding and work in your life the way He sees fit.

I will use certain people who don't know Me personally, events, circumstances and tools to further My work and for your blessing. Don't be surprised when I do this. I work through whomever I want and is at My disposal. I do this in order to teach you that My work goes beyond human limitations and comprehension.

"The voice spoke from heaven a second time, 'Do not call anything impure that God has made clean.'" – Acts 11:9

I assure you that there were many widows in Israel in Elijah's time, when the sky was shut for three and a half years and there was a severe famine throughout the land. Yet Elijah was not sent to any of them, but to a widow in Zarephath in the region of Sidon. – Luke 4:25-26

To the person who pleases him, God gives wisdom, knowledge and happiness, but to the sinner he gives the task of gathering and storing up wealth to hand it over to the one who pleases God. This too is meaningless, a chasing after the wind. – Ecclesiastes 2:26

18

SHIELD OF FAITH

In addition to all this, take up the shield of faith, with which you can extinguish all the flaming arrows of the evil one. – Ephesians 6:16

Sooner or later, the Evil One's arrows will fly toward you. If you're not ready for battle, they will injure you. Start preparing your shield of faith now and learn how to use it to stop all of the Evil One's arrows.

In olden times, besieging armies often used skilled archers to open the attack. Before launching the arrows, many times they were dipped in tar and set afire to cause even more damage wherever they landed. Those defending themselves against the flying missiles would cover up with shields greased in olive oil to prevent the leather-covered wooden shields from bursting into flames.

In the spiritual war, arrows of worries, sorrows and uncertainty fly toward the believer, who must carry the shield of faith as protection. This shield will help block the arrows that the Evil One launches.

To keep the shield of faith rendering the arrows harmless and from bursting into flames, we must cover it with the oil of the Holy Spirit. Meditation in the presence of God, prayer, and singing praises will both anoint and bring a fresh layer of oil over our faith. We will annihilate the arrow of worry by utilizing the shield of faith. We can paralyze the doubt attacking our mind through faith. With faith, we will block the Evil One's attacks on us and our home. When we spend time in the presence of God, the shield of faith will harden and become easy to wield in the daily battles that we will face.

Wield the shield of faith every day, and I will give you strength in the battles that you face during this time. Perhaps right now you can't see the Evil One's arrows as he prepares them to launch them against you, but I see them. I see his plans, and that is why I want to prepare you to be victorious and put him to shame. Guard the shield of faith and anoint it with the Holy Spirit's oil in order to render the Evil One's arrows harmless. I will give you victory. Don't forget that I am with you, and I surround you from every side like a shield. Trust Me in sunny times and in difficult ones."

*But you, L*ORD*, are a shield around me, my glory, the One who lifts my head high. – Psalm 3:3*

They set the tables, they spread the rugs, they eat, they drink! Get up, you officers, oil the shields! – Isaiah 21:5

For everyone who has been born of God overcomes the world. And this is the victory that has overcome the world—our faith. – 1 John 5:4 (ESV)

19

PUT YOUR PROBLEM BEFORE ME

Hezekiah received the letter from the messengers and read it. Then he went up to the temple of the LORD and spread it out before the LORD. - 2 Kings 19:14

When a difficult problem comes in your path, you will look for solutions to solve it. You will retreat within yourself to meditate on the problem and will seek the counsel of others to find a solution. In time, you will notice that some problems are beyond your human ability to solve and focusing on these problems will only steal your inner peace and trouble your mind.

Remember that, through God all things are possible. He can see your sorrow from above and can show you the solution. There is a way to attain peace in the middle of the storm. When you let the light of His presence into your life, you will see how peace settles down over you—even if the problem persists.

King Hezekiah received a threatening letter from a powerful army. In one moment, when the situation became extremely overwhelming, Hezekiah took the letter before God and spoke to Him about the sorrow the message caused him. God spoke to the prophet Isaiah, telling him to take a message to Hezekiah and lift him up from his state of heaviness.

In the midst of problems and news that will often overwhelm you, you will have to take the letter full of your tears before God and show Him. Speak to Him and tell Him what is bothering you. Relinquish your worries and sorrows to Him and stay in His presence until He pours peace and certainty into your heart. He is in control and will bring you a solution soon. Learn to leave your daily worries before Him and receive His perfect peace.

I know that sometimes you will try to solve certain difficult problems, and you will feel lost and alone, as in a maze. Your mind will seek solutions in every direction, and sometimes the solution will not be found because they are beyond your power. But don't forget that I am beyond your limitations and human walls. If you bring your problems before Me, I can solve them beyond your ability to understand. I can light your path and guide you. Put the situation before Me, speak to Me, take My advice, make your time with Me a priority and My presence will light the darkness of all the problems you face.

I have told you these things, so that in me you may have peace. In this world you will have trouble. But take heart! I have overcome the world. – John 16:33

Who of you by worrying can add a single hour to your life? Since you cannot do this very little thing, why do you worry about the rest? – Luke 12:25-26

20

ASK ME BEFORE DECIDING

Call to me and I will answer you and tell you great and unsearchable things you do not know. – Jeremiah 33:3

Life is made up of daily decisions that you must make. Each decision you make is like a railroad turnout that sends the train from one track to another at a junction. Oftentimes, appearances will deceive you; many things you see will reflect only one side of reality, and you will need divine discovery to understand before deciding. God sees far beyond what you can see, and He wants to guide you to make the best decisions for your present and future. Therefore, you should remain in constant connection with Him. Discipline yourself to listen to His whisper, and He will help you choose the path leading to blessing.

A group of poorly dressed people with inadequate food and drink came to Joshua, seeking an alliance. They had come from a faraway land and had heard of the Israelites' powerful God. Unfortunately, their appearance and lack of provisions was all an act—a deception about who they were. Joshua agreed to the alliance without praying and asking for God's divine guidance. Thus, he fell into the trap and formed an alliance with the Gibeonite people, which led to losing certain blessings. The deceivers were, in fact, the very enemies they were trying to defeat!

God sees beyond what our eyes see. He knows in which

direction circumstances will unfold and how the future will look. When we must make an important decision, we need to ask Him and seek His point of view on our situation. God will light our mind to see beyond appearances; He can remind us of a spiritual principle, give us a sign or a message to help us make the right decision. The more we stay close to Him, the more we will be able to develop the ability to filter decisions through the perspective of divine principles and make good decisions based on His will. God's perspective will take us to the best pastures and restful waters, but we must stay in close connection with Him in order to hear His guiding whisper.

You will receive some attractive offers in the upcoming period, but they will not all be from Me. Some of them are attractive traps to deceive you, but if you stay in close connection with Me, I will reveal to you what decision you must make. I have blessings prepared that I am ready to give you, and I want to lead you to them. The steps you must take, even if they are new for you, will be through faith and toward green pastures and restful waters. Ask Me, and I will guide you.

And this is my prayer: that your love may abound more and more in knowledge and depth of insight, so that you may be able to discern what is best and may be pure and blameless for the day of Christ. – Philippians 1:9-10

He reveals deep and hidden things; he knows what lies in darkness, and light dwells with him. – Daniel 2:22

21

ANGER CAN AFFECT YOUR FUTURE

Whoever is slow to anger is better than the mighty,
and he who rules his spirit than he who takes a city.
– Proverbs 16:32 (ESV)

Uncontrolled anger can lead a person to take actions that he or she will later regret. Do not allow anger to stain your future or destroy His glorious plan for your life. These moments of animosity can destroy everything you have built thus far. Anger can push you into committing unthinkable acts; it can defeat the wisdom you have accumulated thus far and destroy your honor.

Nabal, whose name means "fool," treated David badly, offending him and acting unjustly. Blinded by anger because of his unjust treatment, David, who had done nothing but good to this man, gathered his friends to take bitter revenge and destroy all that belonged to Nabal. Upon hearing of her husband's injustice toward David, Abigail, a beautiful and wise woman, decided to act, taking David all that he had requested of her husband. She bowed before the future king and said, "Don't take Nabal seriously, because true to his name, he acted hastily and foolishly. When God fulfills the plan He has for you and you become king, your conscience will not cause you any trouble for spilling innocent blood."

Abigail was warning David that if he let himself be dominated by anger and destroyed Nabal *and his household,* he was making a mistake that would be like a dark stain on his past The bright future God had prepared for him would be affected negatively. David wisely heeded the plea of Nabal's wife Abigail. Likewise, the plan that He has for you can be ruined by the anger that can discredit you. Do not add another link to the chain of revenge. Leave the problem in God's hands. He is the judge who will do justice for you; He will repay everyone, and He is your defender.

When you are treated unjustly and provoked, do not respond. Do not let yourself act upon the rising wave of anger and do unthinkable things that will remain like a stain on your past. My plan is beautiful, glorious, unimaginable for you, but do not ruin it in a fit of anger. Pray before Me to give you self-control. I am the judge who will reward you and do justice for you. Revenge is Mine. Do not put yourself on the judge's bench. I love you, and I will do justice for you.

When the Lord has fulfilled for my Lord every good thing he promised concerning him and has appointed him ruler over Israel, my Lord will not have on his conscience the staggering burden of needless bloodshed or of having avenged himself. And when the Lord your God has brought my Lord success, remember your servant."
– 1 Samuel 25:30-31

For we know him who said, "It is mine to avenge; I will repay," and again, "The Lord will judge his people."
– Hebrews 10:30

As dead flies give perfume a bad smell, so a little folly outweighs wisdom and honor.
– Ecclesiastes 10:1

22

THE PRAYER YOU LIFT UP WILL BRIGHTEN YOUR LIFE

I call to you, LORD, come quickly to me; hear me when I call to you. May my prayer be set before you like incense; may the lifting up of my hands be like the evening sacrifice. – Psalm 141:1-2

The prayer you lift up within your soul or out loud has an unseen aroma/fragrance. This scent has the power to brighten your sorrowful spiritual environment and to bring you joy. The prayer is the incense that transforms the smell of life's sorrows.

When the prophet prepared the censer for prayer, it contained hot coals over which the incense was spread. This mixture of five spices produced a pleasant aroma that filled the room.

Life will often bring "hot coals" that will be difficult to handle. The hot coals might be a disease, a financial crisis, a failure or other pain-filled trials. These struggles are the coals that will often appear in your life's censer. What you can do is place the incense, which symbolizes prayer, over the hot coals. This combination will create a pleasant scent that will purify your life before God, and His peace will spread over you. With your prayers, produce a pleasant scent within your life's circumstances that are oftentimes sorrowful.

Speak to Me. Tell Me about your pain and let Me help you through the circumstances you are experiencing. Put them before Me, and I will take care of them. I will sweeten the situation you are undergoing. Through faith and dialogue with Me, a pleasant aroma will rise up, sweeten your life's sorrows, and help you go through this difficult time. Thank Me through faith because I can resolve your situation even if you do not see any solution.

The smoke of the incense, together with the prayers of God's people, went up before God from the angel's hand.
– Revelation 8:4

Follow God's example, therefore, as dearly loved children and walk in the way of love, just as Christ loved us and gave himself up for us as a fragrant offering and sacrifice to God. – Ephesians 5:1-2

Perfume and incense bring joy to the heart, and the pleasantness of a friend springs from their heartfelt advice.
– Proverbs 27:9

23

GOD IS YOUR DEFENDER

I depend on God alone; I put my hope in him. He alone protects and saves me; he is my defender, and I shall never be defeated. My salvation and honor depend on God; he is my strong protector; he is my shelter. – Psalm 62:5-7 (GNT).

Have you ever gone through times when you were treated unjustly? Were you hurt by the situation? Did you feel sorrow? May I assure you that God is the defender of His children? He is the One who intervenes and does justice beyond expectations. Man's intention is to bring revenge on those who did him wrong, but God expects you not to sit on the judge's bench. God wants you to let Him judge as He knows best.

Joseph's brothers envied him because his father had made him a garment that showed his favoritism toward Rachel's son. Their envy and jealousy drove them to sell him into slavery. Painful, right? Even if, in appearance, Joseph's brothers had won, God did not leave things as they had arranged them. After years, Joseph became vice-pharaoh in Egypt, the most powerful kingdom of that time. When a global crisis hit the land, Joseph acted with kindness and saved his betraying brothers from death by starvation. He helped them reestablish themselves in the country that he led. A nice ending to the story, right?

Jacob, now in his old age and living in Egypt, called for Joseph and his two sons, saying, "The two that were born here in Egypt, I will adopt, they will be mine. I will name them in my inheritance, and they will have equal rights to my other children."

God became Joseph's defender and gave Joseph double through his sons. He is your defender as well. Even if others have harmed you, know that the Heavenly Father has plans to defend you and turn the situation in your favor. The best Advocate and Judge is on your side. Wait and you will see.

When someone does you wrong, do not seek revenge. Revenge is Mine. Let Me fight for you. I am the Defender. I am the Judge. You fight with the weapons of blamelessness, and I will turn the situation to your favor. Watch Me at work. Do not let yourself be defeated by sorrow, but thank Me, for I will turn the situation to your favor. Wait in faith so that I may do justice for you.

The LORD says to my lord: "Sit at my right hand until I make your enemies a footstool for your feet."
– Psalm 110:1

Now then, your two sons born to you in Egypt before I came to you here will be reckoned as mine; Ephraim and Manasseh will be mine, just as Reuben and Simeon are mine. Any children born to you after them will be yours; in the territory they inherit they will be reckoned under the names of their brothers. – Genesis 48:5-6

24

Live in Freedom and Not in Accusation

He canceled the record of the charges against us and took it away by nailing it to the cross. – Colossians 2:14 (NLT)

Even though many people are free, they live in accusation. This blame they feel is like an obstacle that stops the wheel of the chariot of victory from moving forward. The Evil One brings these accusations into the mind and soul to bring sorrow and steal joy.

In the time of the apostle Paul when the accused person was imprisoned, a handwritten parchment, stating the allegations and charges against the accused would be posted at the door of his cell. That parchment reminded the person of the past and his bleak future.

When the Lord Jesus died on the cross, He took the parchment with the charges and accusations against every man and nailed them to the cross. When He was crucified, His blood dripped over the parchment and erased every man's blame. Any accusation and charge were paid for on the cross.

Accept the freedom earned by His sacrifice on the cross and proclaim it over your life. Thank God that it comes from Him and don't let the Evil One to dig through the past and launch accusations against you that bring sorrow and steal your joy.

God has forgiven you; He has cleansed you, and you are free. Accept forgiveness, proclaim it over your life and live as a free man. Living in freedom brings joy, and God's joy will be your strength.

When accusing thoughts knock on your mind's door, proclaim the forgiveness you have received. I have given you forgiveness, freedom, and I love you. I want you to live a life full of joy and freedom; I want you to walk with your head high. Do not accept the blame that the Evil One whispers to you. I want you to proclaim the freedom that I have earned for you on the cross and to walk now filled with the joy of forgiveness.

So if the Son sets you free, you will be free indeed.
– John 8:36

Therefore, there is now no condemnation for those who are in Christ Jesus. – Romans 8:1

If we confess our sins, he is faithful and just and will forgive us our sins and purify us from all unrighteousness. – 1 John 1:9

25

PRIVATE VICTORIES WILL PROPEL YOU

*Benaiah son of Jehoiada from Kabzeel was another fa-
mous soldier… He once went down into a pit on a snowy
day and killed a lion.* – 2 Samuel 23:20 (GNT)

What you do in private will affect your public life.
The victories you reach when no one sees you will
propel you in your social life, bringing you recognition. Each
victory you have is like another brick added to your castle of
victory. Any victory over temptation, trials and wish to live
without boundaries will bring God's blessings over you.

Young Benaiah faced a lion that crossed his path during the
winter days. He embraced a tough battle against the king of all
animals. The young man came out victorious, but people did
not see the battle. When King David was looking for someone
to be the leader of his personal guard, Benaiah was appointed
for that important position. King David chose him because he
had also fought against a lion and knew what was needed to
triumph in such a battle. What young Benaiah had earned in
private trampolined him to a special position in public life.

Oftentimes, fighting battles when no one sees you or ap-
preciates you will be hard to do. Don't forget: God sees your
struggle and battles and will repay you. Keep being disciplined
and as you continue to invest in your future, all of these small

victories will eventually catapult you to a coveted position. Do not step back; keep going with faith, and your work will be repaid.

I will bring your personal victories out from hiding and display them in public. Keep fighting, hold on to your integrity, and let yourself be guided by your Holy Spirit. A time will come when your personal victories will be a great blessing for you, but that is what I control. You keep fighting, and I will place your victor's crown on your head.

Blessed is the one who perseveres under trial because, having stood the test, that person will receive the crown of life that the Lord has promised to those who love him. – James 1:12

But thank God! He gives us victory over sin and death through our Lord Jesus Christ. – 1 Corinthians 15:57

For everyone who has been born of God overcomes the world. And this is the victory that has overcome the world—our faith. – 1 John 5:4 (ESV)

26

THE THOUGHTS YOU FEED LEAD THE WAY

For as he thinks in his heart, so is he. –Proverbs 23:7 (NKJV)

Many thoughts, both good and bad, constantly flit through your mind. Each of them will attempt to take root and develop. The thoughts that your mind feeds are the precursors to the actions you will take, which will also give your life direction.

If you entertain positive thoughts, then your attitudes will be positive and full of hope. If you ruminate on negative thoughts, then the good things will be distorted as you look at them through a negative lens. Negative news has a way of drawing you in and capturing your attention. Consuming these thoughts will cause you to feel as though you are on an emotional roller coaster that runs continuously without accomplishing anything. Negative news steals your joy and peace that comes from God's presence.

The mind must be renewed in order to live a life of victory. If thoughts are dominated by the negative and by wrong ideas, you will not walk in the Holy Spirit. You can renew your mind in the Word of God by reading it, mediating on it and living it. Thus, the negative thought paradigms will be confronted and will not be allowed to take hold in the fertile field of your mind. If you don't push them away when they insistently knock on your mind's door, they will sabotage your joy and life of victory. Let the holy Word mold your mind and thoughts and thus you will receive hope.

Decide today to give your mind the messages of the Word that can make the Holy Ghost connect them with the situations you are experiencing, and they may provide you with a resolution and guidance. The Holy Ghost working in close connection with the Holy Word can create a life full of victory and meaning.

My Spirit must be at your mind's gate to check and filter every thought. Fight the negative thoughts with My help. Make them obey Christ. Sow My Word in the fertile field of your mind. Rely on it and, in time, you will notice that you will live a life of victory and joy, and my Spirit will guide you daily in what you have to do. The channel linking you and Me will be open, and I will be able to constantly whisper to you.

Do not conform to the pattern of this world but be transformed by the renewing of your mind. Then you will be able to test and approve what God's will is—his good, pleasing and perfect will. – Romans 12:2

We demolish arguments and every pretension that sets itself up against the knowledge of God, and we take captive every thought to make it obedient to Christ.
– 2 Corinthians 10:5

27

LOOK AT ME MORE THAN AT THE WAVES

"Come," he said. Then Peter got down out of the boat, walked on the water and came toward Jesus. But when he saw the wind, he was afraid and, beginning to sink, cried out, "LORD, save me!" Immediately Jesus reached out his hand and caught him. "You of little faith," he said, "why did you doubt?" – Matthew 14:29-31

For a person to leave his or her comfort space is like descending from a boat in the middle of the water. Taking a step of faith is like walking in the unknown. Trust me, you will need faith and courage. You will always have to look at Jesus to gain the strength to proceed forward. That is the place where you will best be able to see the manifestation of His power.

Peter remained on the pages of the Bible as the man who walked on water because he was brave enough to do so when the Lord replied, "Yes, come." But he began to sink as soon as he took his eyes off Jesus to look at the wind and waves around him. Like Peter, the moment we remove our eyes from Jesus will be the moment when walking through the unknown becomes difficult.

Perhaps you have also taken the step of faith that surpasses your familiar comfort zone. You also did that when you heard the Lord's voice saying, "Yes, come." However, now you are looking at the waves of adversity that are rising around you, and discouragement is enveloping you. The more you look at the waves, the more you will take your attention from God. Look instead at His hand that is ready to catch you and help you. Do not let the howling of the wind be stronger in your ear than God's voice whispering, "I will support you with My victorious hand."

Look more at Jesus who is walking above the waves and coming to help you. He wants to manifest His power among the waves of life that you are experiencing, and He wants to offer His experience and the testimony of His intervention.

I would like you to keep your gaze more on Me—not on the waves. I will tell you how to step and where to go. Listen to My directions. I will take your hand when the trials are difficult. Do not listen to what your friends in the boat say, for they have not taken the step of faith. Look and listen at what I tell you, and that is how you will get ahead. Listen to My voice more than the voice of the wind. The time spent in My presence will strengthen you, and I will light your path and show you how to continue going forward.

And let us run with perseverance the race marked out for us, fixing our eyes on Jesus, the pioneer and perfecter of faith. For the joy set before him he endured the cross,

scorning its shame, and sat down at the right
hand of the throne of God.
– Hebrew 12:1-2

When Jesus woke up, he rebuked the wind and said
to the waves, "Silence! Be still!" Suddenly the wind
stopped, and there was a great calm. Then he asked
them, "Why are you afraid? Do you still have no faith?"
The disciples were absolutely terrified.
"Who is this man?" they asked each other.
"Even the wind and waves obey him!"
– Mark 4:39-41 (NLT)

28

LIFT UP THE DEFEATED

But a Samaritan, as he traveled, came where the man was; and when he saw him, he took pity on him. He went to him and bandaged his wounds, pouring on oil and wine. Then he put the man on his own donkey, brought him to an inn and took care of him. – Luke 10:33-34

I will bring people around you who are defeated, and you will need to uplift them.

Many people will cross your path in life. Some will namelessly pass by you, but with others you will spend more time. You will notice that some of them will have been defeated by sadness and carry multiple sorrows in their soul. Your role will be to apply ointment on their wounds. You will have to use your spiritual gifts and the abilities that I have given you to uplift them. They need to receive the hope I have for them through you.

Joseph was unjustly accused and imprisoned. The king's unjustly accused cupbearer was in the same prison. When he and the baker were sharing their dreams, Joseph approached them and lifted up the cupbearer by interpreting his dream. He told him that in three days he would be released from prison. After two years, their roles were reversed. God used the cupbearer to bring Joseph before Pharaoh where he was also set free. Lift up those around you and you, in turn, will be uplifted. At some point, you will be blessed through those you have helped.

Today, you will need to be like the Good Samaritan who anointed the wounds of the defeated one to generate healing. Be the extension of God's hand in action. God will bring people around you who need your word of encouragement. Some of those God sends you way will need you to open a door for them, and others will need you to be a mediator for them.

Stay in My presence and speak to Me. I will prepare your soul and show you those who need help. I will open your mind and encourage your spirit so that you will know what to say and how to frame the issue. I will bring people around you who feel defeated, and you will have to pour the healing oil that comes from being in My presence into their souls. Speak to them with confidence because their souls need Me.

So he [Joseph] asked Pharaoh's officials who were in custody with him in his master's house, "Why do you look so sad today?" "We both had dreams," they answered, "but there is no one to interpret them." Then Joseph said to them, "Do not interpretations belong to God? Tell me your dreams." – Genesis 40:6-8 (NLT)

For the Holy Spirit will teach you at that time what you should say. – Luke 12:12

Timely advice is lovely, like golden apples in a silver basket. – Proverbs 25:11 (NLT)

29

TRANSMIT THE RAYS OF HOPE

You are the light of the world. A town built on a hill cannot be hidden. Neither do people light a lamp and put it under a bowl. Instead they put it on its stand, and it gives light to everyone in the house. In the same way, let your light shine before others, that they may see your good deeds and glorify your Father in heaven.
– Matthew 5:14-16

Your life should be a light for those around you. Imagine your life being like a tower atop a mountain from where bright rays of divine presence come. Many people around you often stumble through the valley of sorrow and hopelessness. They walk in the darkness and do not know God, but your actions will light their lives and help them make good decisions in the wilderness of their circumstances.

When you stay in the presence of God, who is the Light of the World, you become filled with light, and the rays of His presence will shine from you. Moses stood in the presence of God on the mountaintop, and when he returned to the people, his face was shining. Likewise, when you stay in His presence, you will be filled with the rays of hope and faith, which will be reflected from you for those around to see and feel.

An abundance of darkness fills the world, but when you

stay connected to the presence of God, you will be filled with light and truth. You will become a guide for those who are in the darkness.

When you stay in the light of My presence, you will see how the light will start to penetrate into all of the nooks of your mind, and the darkness and fear will begin to disappear. My light will light your life even brighter if you entrust your moments of darkness to Me. I will help you see life's circumstances and problems more clearly and to make good decisions guided by Me. For those near you, the light of My presence will manifest through you. Be a great blessing to them and light their darkness with My light. Stay in My presence to stay charged with light.

Make your face shine on your servant and teach me your decrees. – Psalm 119:135

When Moses came down from Mount Sinai with the two tablets of the covenant law in his hands, he was not aware that his face was radiant because he had spoken with the LORD. – Exodus 34:29

In him was life, and that life was the light of all mankind. The light shines in the darkness, and the darkness has not overcome it. – John 1:4-5

30

HIDDEN TREASURES

And I will give you treasures hidden in the darkness—secret riches. I will do this so you may know that I am the LORD, the God of Israel, the one who calls you by name.
– Isaiah 45:3 (NLT)

On this day, the Lord wants to surprise you with various treasures He has sprinkled along the path where you will walk. These treasures will tell you how much He loves you. These valuables are hidden from your eyes, but the light of His presence will reveal them if you spend time with Him and pay close attention.

When the "scales" that covered Saul's eyes fell off at the moment of prayer, he began to clearly see his old life with new eyes. Not all those who have walked alongside him on the road to Damascus had the same experience.

The presence of the Lord brings about the light that chases away the darkness. Only then can you see beyond what is apparent. The light of His presence will reveal your hidden treasures and a new direction. He wants to give you some of these treasures gift-wrapped in unusual ways. Some will come in the form of a trial or in a sudden ending that brings along great blessings. Other riches that He wants to give you will be in the form of beautiful words, an answer to a prayer, a unique opportunity, a friend or other material items. When you stay in the light of His presence, you will notice that your heart's eyes will light up, and you will be able to look beyond appearances. The darkness will disappear, and you will better understand what the Lord wants to give you or do for you.

I can cast aside the darkness and light up your mind's eyes so that you may see. Perhaps you have been praying before Me for a long time for a new step, a change, a new business, and it seems like every door is closed. I have prepared treasures that will amaze you and ones which you will reach for if you allow My light to light your way and if you will receive revelation from Me. I want to open up the eyes of your heart so that you may understand and see beyond appearances.

I pray that the eyes of your heart may be enlightened in order that you may know the hope to which he has called you, the riches of his glorious inheritance in his holy people, and his incomparably great power for us who believe. – Ephesians 1:18-19

He will be the sure foundation for your times, a rich store of salvation and wisdom and knowledge; the fear of the LORD is the key to this treasure. – Isaiah 33:6

31

Joy Comes from Me

To all who mourn in Israel, he will give a crown of beauty for ashes, a joyous blessing instead of mourning, festive praise instead of despair. In their righteousness, they will be like great oaks that the Lord has planted for his own glory. – Isaiah 61:3 (NLT)

You were created by the Lord to rejoice. The state of joy is part of His ongoing plan for your life.

Joy is a fruit of the Holy Spirit that is produced in your life when you live according to His will. If you sow His promises in your heart, they will bring you rest in the midst of trials. Many people try to manufacture joy through various worldly means, i.e., material possessions, social standing, unheard-of experiences. But when you adopt this method to find pleasure, the dose must continually increase for satisfaction to be produced. The joy that comes from the Lord is a fruit of the Spirit that comes about after walking in His paths and promises.

A different joy sets into your life in the moment when God takes your burden of tears and pain and transforms it into joy. His answers to the prayers you've long had will bring an indescribable state of joy. He wants to pour joy into your life and to change your cry to a song of joy.

The accusing thoughts that the Evil One brings into your

mind will taint the oil of joy. Past accusations are meant to bring the shadows of regret and extinguish the flames of joy and enthusiasm like messengers of the Evil One. Do not allow accusations to live in your mind's chamber. Of course, even the Holy Spirit will shine the light of the Word over certain aspects that you must change. His purpose is to clean the oil to freshen it.

I want to light the flame of joy and enthusiasm in your life even brighter. The joy I will pour over you will be at the soul level, and it will spill over in all aspects of your life. Pray before Me so that nothing will block your joy. Many feel sorrow because their life's joy is blocked. I want to surprise you in the time to come and undo some of the sorrows you have long carried. The time has come to transform your cry into a song of praise. Walk confidently on this day and spread My joy over those you meet.

You have loved righteousness and hated wickedness; therefore God, your God, has set you above your companions by anointing you with the oil of joy.
– Hebrews 1:9

May the God of hope fill you with all joy and peace as you trust in him, so that you may overflow with hope by the power of the Holy Spirit.
– Romans 15:13

32

A Window of Opportunity

Making the most of every opportunity, because the days are evil. – Ephesians 5:16

Expect great opportunities to cross your path. Those that God brings your way constitute one of the ways in which He offers you blessings. You can also express your love for Him through these circumstances. Opportunities are like trains that stop at your life's station. Sadly, if you allow them to pass, they will never return.

If you have divine light and wisdom, you will know how to use the opportunities that come into your life. You must develop your spiritual sensitivity to understand which of the opportunities are sent by God and which are the traps of the Evil One. Pray for discernment before favorable opportunities come along your path, and don't allow fear to paralyze you or stop you from going through the door that He opens for you.

Jesus' choosing to enter Simon's home was a unique opportunity for Simon to benefit from His visit by honoring Jesus. However, he did not even follow the social etiquette of that time by offering Jesus a basin of water to wash His dusty feet. Instead, a sinful woman saw the opportunity to pour an expensive perfume on His feet, honoring Him with her gift of love. Jesus praised her, and her act of selflessness remains an example for all of us to follow.

God will open doors through which you will be able to express your love toward Him and toward those who are close to you. He will give you opportune moments when you will be able to grow in faith or through which to do something for His kingdom. Bartimaeus, the blind man, had his moment when Jesus passed by on his street. Bartimaeus took advantage of the situation and yelled with all his might, asking to be healed and for Jesus to save him. Those around him asked him to be quiet, but Bartimaeus knew this was his only opportunity to take advantage of Jesus' healing powers. Blind Bartimaeus was healed and began to see—physically and spiritually—because he did not let that unique opportunity pass him by.

I will bring opportunities before you to serve Me and show Me your love. I will bless you through circumstances I will bring before you and surprise you with what I want to give you. Do not neglect what comes in your path; be attentive because I send them with a purpose. When you see the blessing that will come over you, you will have to admit before Me and others that My hand blessed you— not luck or a matter of coincidence.

Then he turned toward the woman and said to Simon, "Do you see this woman? I came into your house. You did not give me any water for my feet, but she wet my feet with her tears and wiped them with her hair."
– Luke 7:44

You did not put oil on my head, but she has poured perfume on my feet.
– Luke 7:46

Therefore, as we have opportunity, let us do good to all people, especially to those who belong to the family of believers.
– Galatians 6:10

33

GOD WILL FIGHT FOR YOU

The LORD will fight for you; you need only to be still.
– Exodus 14:14

In this world, no one will be exempt from problems. Sometimes they will come like crests of waves—one after another, trying to sink you. Most often, God will surround you with a protective shield, and other times He will fight for you. Even if you do not see His assistance with your physical eyes, He is the One who guards you and sends His angels to fight battles for you. Be calm in the storm, and you will surely see His salvation.

Elisha's house was surrounded by the foreign armies seeking to destroy it. When Elisha's servant, Gehazi, went out in the morning, he saw the hills full of the armies that were battle ready. He became frightened by the less-than-favorable circumstances, but Elisha, full of confidence, prayed for Gehazi so that the Lord would open his eyes and enable him to see beyond what his human eyes could see. He saw the skies full of riders on horseback, chariots of fire and heavenly armies ready to join the action and fight for them.

Perhaps you also go through times when you feel like the Evil One has set his cannons on your home and family. He is shooting projectile after projectile—problem after problem. The time has come to pray to God to open your eyes so that you may see God's armies ready to act and protect you. His armies are ready to march toward you and form a protective shield against the problems that the Evil One catapults toward you. God is your shield; He is your escape tower where you can hide.

I want you to thank Me on this day for the protection I have provided you thus far. I will continue to guard you from the Evil One's attacks. Reflect more on My power and less on problems. The more you will stay in My presence, the more clearly you will see the skies full of My armies ready to intervene for you. Make Me your escape tower. I am your shield in every circumstance, and I will protect you because I love you.

And Elisha prayed, "Open his eyes, LORD, so that he may see." Then the LORD opened the servant's eyes, and he looked and saw the hills full of horses and chariots of fire all around Elisha. – 2 Kings 6:17

If you say, "The LORD is my refuge," and you make the Most High your dwelling, no harm will overtake you, no disaster will come near your tent. For he will command his angels concerning you to guard you in all your ways. – Psalm 91:9-11 (NLT)

"I have told you these things, so that in me you may have peace. In this world you will have trouble. But take heart! I have overcome the world." – John 16:33

34

DETOURS WILL TURN INTO BLESSINGS

His father was sick in bed, suffering from fever and dysentery. Paul went in to see him and, after prayer, placed his hands on him and healed him. When this had happened, the rest of the sick on the island came and were cured. – Acts 28:8-9

People make plans for upcoming years. They follow an exact plan because they want to reach a certain goal. Perhaps you also have a goal that you want to reach.

However, sometimes, a detour comes into your life who simply derails you from your goal for months or years. Detours are frustrating and difficult to understand, but never forget that God is sovereign. Perhaps you do not understand that He sees your life from above and is in control. You find it very difficult to accept what is happening in your life, forgetting that God always wants what is best for you. He never makes mistakes. Even in life's storms that distance you from your aim, you have to accept, through faith, that God has a wonderful plan for your life.

The apostle Paul set Rome as his aim; however, a storm destroyed the ship and their plans. The entire crew was shipwrecked on an island. There, Paul announced the gospel and healed many who were ill. That detour to the island was not a loss, for God had a specific purpose for Paul to aid those who were ill. God's divine plan was to use him to heal and preach the gospel on that island.

You will also experience detours in your life as well. You may not understand the why, but you will have to accept that those times are scheduled by God with great purpose. During life's detours, you will need to continue fulfilling the work He has for you to do. The work will not always be easy or comfortable, but in that time, you will have the opportunity to develop your faith in Him and to rely on His promises.

God also allows detours because He wants to guard you from the traps set by the Evil One. Be attentive to your spiritual level when you are going through a detour, so that you may understand the reason why you are going through a trial. If you cannot understand at the moment, you will surely understand after some time in retrospect.

If life does not go as you have planned and you are now in a detour of life, I want you to know that I have great purpose for this detour. I want to show you something. I want to connect you with My plans. Do not be discouraged! Nothing is lost. You are My child, and I have only the best plans for you. Accept through faith that all things will work together for your good.

For I know the plans I have for you," declares the LORD, "plans to prosper you and not to harm you, plans to give you hope and a future. – Jeremiah 29:11

So do not fear, for I am with you; do not be dismayed,
for I am your God. I will strengthen you and help you; I
will uphold you with my righteous right hand.
– Isaiah 41:10

35

HE WILL TAKE CARE OF YOU

But seek first his kingdom and his righteousness, and all these things will be given to you as well. Therefore do not worry about tomorrow, for tomorrow will worry about itself. Each day has enough trouble of its own. – Matthew 6:33-34

You tend, as all the others do, to worry about tomorrow and the next day. That worry can become so pressing that it becomes much like a thief stealing the peace and joy from your heart.

The pressing image of tomorrow or of the bleak future you imagine is due to the absence of God from the image that your mind is creating. You visualize problems or think of what might appear on the horizon, but you do not put the presence of the Almighty God in the image that is in your mind.

When you begin to worry, put the image of the Almighty God on His throne in the midst of your problems. See how rays of light full of power shine from His throne lighting every corner. See how the tails of His cloak fill the whole earth and the angels sing around the throne of glory, ready to get into the action to help you.

Insert the image of the Almighty God into any image that your mind creates of the problems that you have, and your fear will go away.

Thank Me because I have always been beside you, and I have kept you in My palm. Let your mind see My throne of glory and praise, full of power and goodness. Transfer this image into the midst of your problems and proclaim that I am on your side to help you. Thank Me because today I will be on your side. Go forward into the day you are facing with confidence. Pray, thank Me, and receive faith as a result.

Be strong and courageous. Do not be afraid or terrified because of them, for the LORD your God goes with you; he will never leave you nor forsake you.
– Deuteronomy 31:6

In the year that King Uzziah died, I saw the LORD, high and exalted, seated on a throne; and the train of his robe filled the temple. Above him were seraphim, each with six wings: With two wings they covered their faces, with two they covered their feet, and with two they were flying. And they were calling to one another: "Holy, holy, holy is the LORD Almighty; the whole earth is full of his glory." At the sound of their voices the door-posts and thresholds shook and the temple was filled with smoke. – Isaiah 6:1-4

36

MATURING

When I was a child, I talked like a child, I thought like a child, I reasoned like a child. When I became a man, I put the ways of childhood behind me. – 1 Corinthians 13:11

In time, your spiritual development will bring a deeper understanding. Chances are when a child first looks at a syringe, a medicinal needle or a medication, he will see them as playthings or knickknacks. On the other hand, in a doctor's eyes, the syringe, the needle and the medications are the means to save a life.

When you are beginning your spiritual process, you will only have a partial understanding of certain situations—much like looking through the eyes of a spiritual child. But as you grow in faith and knowledge, you will understand more deeply how you can apply the truths of the holy Word. Some things will only make sense when you begin to make connections between things or ideas. You will understand that certain events, even if they seem negative, will turn for your good in God's plan. All things work together for the good of those who love God.

On this earth, in whatever stage of life you might be, you will never fully understand all things. Only when you are in heaven will you fully understand. As for now, you will only know a part, but you need a greater trust in God in the midst of the unknown. Whether you are at the beginning of your race on the path of faith or an experienced Christian, you need to continue the maturing process. Likewise, in life's difficult moments, you need to trust that God will turn things for your good.

I am on your side, I will supervise you, and I will guide you like a good father. I want to show you certainties that hold weight and impact. In order to understand them, you must first work on perfecting yourself to accept the maturing process taking place through the trials you will experience in life. You will be surprised when I show you the reality as I see it, and you will be surprised when I will help you look beyond appearances. What I do for you is for your good—even if you don't understand. My will is difficult to accept at times but trust in Me.

Their responsibility is to equip God's people to do his work and build up the church, the body of Christ. Then we will no longer be immature like children. We won't be tossed and blown about by every wind of new teaching. We will not be influenced when people try to trick us with lies so clever, they sound like the truth.
– Ephesians 4:12, 14 (NLT)

Like newborn babies, crave pure spiritual milk, so that by it you may grow up in your salvation, now that you have tasted that the Lord is good.
– 1 Peter 2:2-3

37

MY WORD WILL NOT RETURN FRUITLESS

As the rain and the snow come down from heaven, and do not return to it without watering the earth and making it bud and flourish, so that it yields seed for the sower and bread for the eater, so is my word that goes out from my mouth: It will not return to me empty, but will accomplish what I desire and achieve the purpose for which I sent it. - Isaiah 55:10-11

His Word, which is alive and true, will transform and bear fruit wherever it goes.

When you look at your life, you can see how the Lord's Word bore fruit. You know the times when it uplifted you, guided you when you didn't know which way to go, and saved you from the sea of sins. You enjoy these truths that now have value in your life. When you go through various stages, you are used to being in His Presence and He, with His light, chases away the shadows of doubt. Every time you choose His Presence, you are allowing the seeds of the Word to be planted in your life and bear fruit that you can enjoy and those around you will also enjoy.

The Word of the Lord is a great treasure—the secret to the kingdom that helps you enjoy and live your life differently.

Drop the Word of the Lord like pearls into the depths of the hearts of those around you who need them so much. Many live in spiritual poverty and in sorrow, but when you plant the seeds of His divine Words, they will bear fruit that you will also get to enjoy at some point.

Proclaim My promises over your life. Make it so My Word may fall over your life like a summer rain to refresh your soul. Proclaim It, accept It, and wait for My promises to be fulfilled. Place the pearls of My Words today in the lives of those around you who live in spiritual poverty and who do not know that joy and fulfillment come from Me. Today, place a pearl in the heart of one who sorrows, and I will repay you!

You gave abundant showers, O God; you refreshed your weary inheritance. – Psalm 68:9

You, God, are my God, earnestly I seek you; I thirst for you, my whole being longs for you, in a dry and parched land where there is no water.
– Psalm 63:1

As the deer pants for streams of water, so my soul pants for you, my God. My soul thirsts for God, for the living God. When can I go and meet with God?
– Psalm 42:1-2

38

THE RAYS OF PEACE

The fruit of that righteousness will be peace; its effect will be quietness and confidence forever. My people will live in peaceful dwelling places, in secure homes, in undisturbed places of rest. – Isaiah 32:17-18

A life lived alongside the Lord does not automatically mean immunity to the storms. Sometimes, the problems will rush over your life in wave after wave but keep fighting to hold your peace. You must be like a lighthouse standing strong in the midst of the waves hitting you.

Peace of mind comes when you bring your problems before Me. In order to have calm and peace, you will have to make quiet in your life even in the midst of storms to listen for His whisper. Proclaim His Word over any tumultuous situations and affirm: "The Almighty God surrounds me with a shield."

Put every task you have to complete before Him today. Some are easy, others are difficult, but present them to Him in prayer. Don't rush to leave His presence. Stay until the Lord floods your mind's chamber with the rays of hope. Read the promises of the Word and let them descend deep into your heart and encourage you. Imagine how they will come true. Let the window of the soul be open in His presence so that the rays of hope coming from Him may get in. After you receive peace and the confidence that He is on your side and will help you, be grateful. Thank Him for resolving your situation, and as peace flows through your life like a peaceful river, you will go from power to power.

When you present your tasks before Me, I will guide you on how to handle them best and fastest. Do not let your full agenda worry you because worry defeats the soul. I love you, I will help you, and I will fill your heart with peace. Bring your sorrows to My attention through prayer, requests, and gratitude. Wait in My presence until your soul is filled with peace. Open the door to your soul so that My rays of hope that are full of power may enter, strengthen, and illuminate you.

"I have told you these things, so that in me you may have peace. In this world you will have trouble. But take heart! I have overcome the world." – John 16:33

Do not be anxious about anything, but in every situation, by prayer and petition, with thanksgiving, present your requests to God. And the peace of God, which transcends all understanding, will guard your hearts and your minds in Christ Jesus. – Philippians 4:6-7

39

GIFTS SPRINKLED ALONG YOUR PATH

Every good and perfect gift is from above, coming down from the Father of the heavenly lights, who does not change like shifting shadows. – James 1:17

The Lord has prepared great and outstanding gifts for you that He wants to give you. These gifts are lasting and will bring about much blessing.

On the other hand, the Enemy imitates the Lord's actions to deceive you. He will bring you gifts that seem attractive, hold many promises, and offer unheard-of joy. However, in the end, his gifts will lead you to ruin. What you must do is distinguish between the gifts that come from the Lord and those that are dangling on the Evil One's hook.

Eve was misled with promises by the Evil One. The gift brought to her was meant to offer her something extraordinary; instead, his "gift" led her to pain in the end. Keep this principle in mind: no gift you receive should ever contradict God's Word.

Some gifts that the Lord will give you will come in unusual packages. Do not reject a gift by simply looking at the package. He will wrap some blessings in the box of trials. You need judgment and wisdom to understand which gifts are from the Heavenly Father.

My gifts to you are good and sublime, and they will lift you up. I have prepared many gifts that I want to place along your path during this time. However, you must be attentive to what the Evil One is offering you as well. Refuse his gifts—even if they appear promising. My Spirit will guide you in all truth. I want you to develop a keenness for the whisper of the Spirit to help you distinguish between gifts.

The blessing of the LORD brings wealth,
without painful toil for it. – Proverbs 10:22

If you, then, though you are evil, know how to give good gifts to your children, how much more will your Father in heaven give good gifts to those who ask him!
– Matthew 7:11

But I am afraid that as the serpent deceived Eve by his cunning, your thoughts will be led astray from a sincere and pure devotion to Christ.
– 2 Corinthians 11:3 (ESV)

40

WINDOWS OF HEAVEN

And God is able to bless you abundantly, so that in all things at all times, having all that you need, you will abound in every good work. – 2 Corinthians 9:8

Sometimes you will feel that life is difficult, and the chariot of victory, which is mired in the mud, will no longer advance forward. Many people have a feeling of being stuck and not moving forward, and their daily toil feels like it goes into a broken bag. Such states of mind cause frustration and pain.

These sorrows must turn your eyes to God, who is the giver of blessings. There is a favor that comes from Him in any season called "the windows of heaven," This favor is pure and simply miraculous. God has windows in heaven that He can open throughout your life at the right time so that He may bless you. A major economic crisis had come to the area where Abraham's son Isaac lived. He thought of moving to another country where there was no crisis. However, God told him to stay where he was despite the famine in the country, telling him that He would bless him. The windows to heaven opened, divine favor was over him that year and, despite the crisis, he was blessed beyond measure.

When you maintain a relationship with Him, He can show

you how to take the next steps and where to be so that His windows may open, and the blessings may pour over you during any time. The rain of blessings will pour over your life, astonishing those around at what He will do for you.

Certainly, the Lord will not waste, but in times of crisis He wants to show you that He can take care of you so that you may enjoy a plentiful life.

I want to surprise you in your time of crisis to come. I will open up the windows to heaven for you, and through them, I will pour blessings over you that you never even expected. When you walk according to My plan and seek My kingdom, I will bless you in ways that you never imagined. Wait and you will see; work and fulfill My plans.

A severe famine now struck the land, as had happened before in Abraham's time.... The Lord appeared to Isaac and said, "Do not go down to Egypt, but do as I tell you." When Isaac planted his crops that year, he harvested a hundred times more grain than he planted, for the Lord blessed him. – Genesis 26:1-2, 12 (NLT)

Bring the whole tithe into the storehouse, that there may be food in my house. Test me in this," says the Lord Almighty, "and see if I will not throw open the floodgates of heaven and pour out so much blessing that there will not be room enough to store it. – Malachi 3:10

41

THROW AWAY WORRY

Therefore do not worry about tomorrow, for tomorrow will worry about itself. Each day has enough trouble of its own. – Matthew 6:34

Worry is like a thick fog that descends over the circumstances of your life. The fog of worry, which is generally unfounded, still frightens many people because it seems impenetrable. However, if you could transform all the fog stretching over various blocks into water, you will see that the thickness only amounts to about a cup of water! The fog seems big, threatening, and dense but, in fact, it is small.

Oftentimes, the fog of worry develops in relation to things that might happen, that seem without solution. Or it can be about things that you are currently experiencing and seemingly have no solution. In these times, a spirit of worry haunts the world—like a shadow over many people's souls.

These shadows can only be extirpated by the Light of His presence. When you allow the Lord's presence to illuminate your life through His promises, you will see how the worry, like fog, dissipates.

Worry is like a circle that many people get into and end up stranded, carried from one danger to another potential troublesome situation. When you try to solve some difficult matters and do not find a solution, do not despair! Absolutely nothing is outside of the Lord's control. He has the power to resolve all your troubles. The Lord has a reputation for turning things around to His children's favor.

Peace settles over you when you stay in the light of His presence and decide to trust in Him. Trusting Him does not mean that problems will disappear, but the more you meditate on the Lord's might and greatness, the more you will realize that worries become minuscule compared to His greatness.

Refusing to worry is proof that you rely on Him who is almighty and sovereign. When you put your problems in His hands, you enter into the Lord's rest. You can live in peace because you have reassurance that He is on your side. The more you carry your problems alone, the greater the sorrow will be.

Sorrows are like a thick fog that settles over your mind and causes you to stumble around. When you spend time in My presence, you will see that My rays of light will penetrate the fog and dissipate it. Bring your sorrows before Me, and I will place an indescribable quiet and a calm over your life—even in the midst of sorrows. My peace will set in over you, and you will move forward confidently.

Look at the birds of the air; they do not sow or reap or store away in barns, and yet your heavenly Father feeds them. Are you not much more valuable than they?
– Matthew 6:26

Cast all your anxiety on him because he cares for you.
– 1 Peter 5:7

Cast your cares on the Lord and he will sustain you;
he will never let the righteous be shaken.
– Psalm 55:22

42

Fight on Both Fronts

Put on the full armor of God, so that you can take your stand against the devil's schemes. – Ephesians 6:11

The battles that you will lead will be on many fronts. Sometimes, you will be tempted to fight more on one front, which will be to the detriment of another. However, in the battles in your life you will lead, the need is to balance each dimension.

Joshua was in the valley fighting physically alongside others. Sometimes, he would advance, other times he would retreat. Moses climbed the mountain and began to pray with his hands held high. When Moses had his hands high, Joshua and the Israelite army would advance, but when exhaustion would force Moses to lower his hands, Joshua would retreat. In the end, Joshua won the physical battle because Moses held his hands high in prayer with the support of two other people—one on each side of him.

The Lord wants you to approach the problems you will encounter in life by fighting on both fronts. Fight to resolve your situation in the physical dimension, but also fight in the spiritual realm through prayer at the same time. Certainly, you will need companions to accompany you in the valley and to accompany you to the mountain in prayer. Maintain a balance between the two realms, and you will advance. Approach the tasks that you have to do on this day by fighting on both fronts. Work to solve them as though it depended only on you, but simultaneously pray before God, as though it totally depended on Him.

When you are going through a difficult situation, stand before Me to receive guidance on how to fight. The Evil One's strategy varies, and that is why when staying in My presence will bring new powers and courage. Speak to Me, look for people to stand with you on the mountain of prayer and people to accompany you in the valley for this is how you will get ahead. Do not neglect the spiritual battle because it affects the physical battle. In My presence, you will receive the power needed to develop the courage to move forward in the battles to fight.

As long as Moses held up his hands, the Israelites were winning, but whenever he lowered his hands, the Amalekites were winning. When Moses' hands grew tired, they took a stone and put it under him and he sat on it. Aaron and Hur held his hands up--one on one side, one on the other--so that his hands remained steady till sunset. So Joshua overcame the Amalekite army with the sword. – Exodus 17:11-13

The horse is made ready for the day of battle, but victory rests with the LORD. – Proverbs 21:31

43

THE LORD IS ON HIS THRONE

In the year that King Uzziah died, I saw the LORD, high and exalted, seated on a throne; and the train of his robe filled the temple. – Isaiah 6:1

In times when life comes crashing down like dominoes, do not forget the God who is in control of the universe has your back. In the moments when life feels like a ship in the middle of an angry ocean, hold tight to the golden reins of hope gleaming through the storm. When the earth's foundations are shaking, do not forget that the Lord is on His throne, and the Anchor of your hope is tied to His throne of grace and endurance, and it is eternal.

The priest Isaiah was disoriented and sad because a good king of Israel had died. He did not know what the future might bring. Would the next king also be a good one or otherwise? Would the new king bring the country into war or be someone who would also seek the face of God? Isaiah, the priest, had questions about his future, as well as his children's and grandchildren's futures. He was disoriented, sad, and filled with a myriad of questions that were throwing him into the abyss of despair. What would happen?

Perhaps you are also going through a period where you don't know which way things will turn from here on. Perhaps you are at a crossroads, perhaps you are in a period of questions, sadness, or perhaps you are battling an illness.

When Isaiah was pressed by questions that he could not answer, he went into the temple to pray, and he saw God sitting on His kingly throne; he saw Him as sovereign over all things and missing nothing from His control. That image revealed to Isaiah helped him receive quiet and peace.

When you stay in His presence, you can take a firmer grip with both hands on the golden reins of hope, and they help you advance through the sands of sadness that try to sink you. You become increasingly aware that the anchor of your faith is tied to the throne of grace and that God is ready to give you grace on this day, so that you may advance victoriously. His greatness chases away worry. His might makes you step with confidence—even if you do not know the future. His love supports you. He is on your side.

> *I reign over and lead this world. Even if you do not understand the situations you experience, I want to remind you that I am beyond time and space. I am sovereign over history. You must look at Me every day to get an increasingly clearer image of My power. See Me on the throne, and your heart will gain confidence and successfully get through the period of questions rolling through your mind, which you have yet to answer. God, who is above the universe, is on your side, and in His time, will change the situation you are going through to your favor. My goodness surrounds you on this day like a shield.*

The LORD sits enthroned over the flood; the LORD is enthroned as King forever. The LORD gives strength to his people; the LORD blesses his people with peace.
– Psalm 29:10-11

We have this hope as an anchor for the soul, firm and secure. It enters the inner sanctuary behind the curtain.
– Hebrews 6:19

Micaiah continued, "Therefore hear the word of the LORD: I saw the LORD sitting on his throne with all the multitudes of heaven standing around him on his right and on his left. – 1 Kings 22:19

44

SPIRITUAL GROWTH OPPORTUNITIES

Consider it pure joy, my brothers and sisters, whenever you face trials of many kinds, because you know that the testing of your faith produces perseverance. Let perseverance finish its work so that you may be mature and complete, not lacking anything. – James 1:2-4

Challenges are the chisels that the Great Sculptor uses for every person's spiritual molding. Pressure, the blow of the hammer, and sorrows do not generate a comfortable atmosphere, and many people tend to avoid challenges. When looking for an exit from a challenge that is meant to mold you, my friend, you are seeking a way out of the school where He placed you to develop you. Consider challenges as opportunities for growth, rather than disasters.

Elimelek and Naomi lived in the time when God allowed a period of famine to turn the nation toward Him. To avoid the difficult time, Elimelek moved his family to a foreign land where everything was plentiful. The Lord allowed a famine to redirect people's gazes toward Him, but Elimelek sought an exit from the challenge. In the land of plenty, Naomi lost her two children, as well as her husband Elimelek, the pillar of the family. Naomi was left alone, but God did not abandon her. Despite the sorrows she experienced, He helped her return to the place she had left and granted her happiness in her old age. The oven of challenges which God allows you to go through has a clear purpose: to mold and uplift you. Even if it hurts and you don't understand why the chisel of challenges and problems hits you, do not forget that God is working toward your development. Perhaps now you are going through hard times; do not sabotage the challenges but seek to find out what the Lord wants to perfect and accomplish in your life. Consider challenges as an opportunity for spiritual growth. Go through the challenges keeping in mind that, at the end, you will be more like the Lord Jesus.

Do not forget that each challenge you will go through has first gone through My hands. I shaped it and allowed it, giving it the proper intensity to reach you. I will not keep you in any challenge for any longer than necessary. What I, as the Sculptor, wants is to mold the vessel of your life, making it useful and honorable for My kingdom. Accept the challenge, consider it an opportunity coming from Me to develop you in the likeness of My Son. Thank Me today through faith for the things that you do not understand as they will work toward your good.

For God knew his people in advance, and he chose them to become like his Son, so that his Son would be the firstborn among many brothers and sisters.
– Romans 8:29 (NLT)

In all this you greatly rejoice, though now for a little while you may have had to suffer grief in all kinds of trials. These have come so that the proven genuineness of your faith--of greater worth than gold, which perishes even though refined by fire--may result in praise, glory and honor when Jesus Christ is revealed.

– 1 Peter 1:6-7

45

THE WAITING ROOM

But those who hope in the LORD will renew their strength. They will soar on wings like eagles; they will run and not grow weary, they will walk and not be faint. – Isaiah 40:31

The waiting room is the place where you must learn to embrace the blessed presence of the Lord. For some, waiting is a frustrating time that leads them to making hasty decisions. But when you wait for particular concerns to happen or a certain event to come, wait with faith that the LORD will show you when to take that next step.

Perhaps you are waiting to start a new job, or to meet the right person, or for something to change in your life. Waiting is difficult when you are without any point of reference, but that time is the right time to get closer to Him, to develop your keenness for hearing His voice and to prepare for the new season in life.

Joseph told the cupbearer he had befriended in prison to put in a good word for him when he was released. However, the cupbearer forgot about him. How sad! Joseph was in the waiting room, and nothing was happening. Two more long and difficult years passed.

When you are in the waiting room and you see that things do not happen in the time that you imagined and that divine promises do not yet materialize for you, do not let discouragement to nest in your soul. While you wait, strengthen yourself in the Lord because He has allowed this period of waiting in order to prepare you for some plan. He has a right time when His plan for you will be fulfilled. Make the waiting room the place where you learn to better distinguish His voice. When the Evil One whispers to you that things will not improve, do not let that same old CD keep replaying in your mind. Rather, proclaim the Lord's goodness toward you and the fact that He has a wonderful plan for you. The waiting room is the place where you can renew your power so that when you leave, you have the strength and clarity necessary to do what the Lord will entrust to you for the next stage of life.

Joseph was released from prison two years after Pharaoh's cupbearer. The Lord appointed him vice-pharaoh so that he could lead the country through a crisis. The waiting room is not the place where you should let the sprouts of sorrow grow or impatience push you to make wrong decisions. The waiting room is the place where you should get closer to God because He wants to prepare you for a new project—a new chapter in your life.

Even if man often forgets about you, know that God will never forget you; He will fulfill the plans He has for your life. Nothing surpasses the time scheduled on the divine calendar. He has wonderful plans for your life—even if you spend some time in the waiting room and have the sense that nothing is happening. At the right time, all of the puzzle pieces will come together.

Trust in Me while you wait. Sometimes you will get the sense that time goes by in vain and that you are not productive. Do not forget I can help you accomplish more in less time when you understand what I have prepared for you. Faith in Me during the waiting time will create an atmosphere of peace and joy in your life. I am preparing you during this time for a new chapter that you will enter. Do not let frustration take hold of you and speak to Me and learn during this time to listen to My voice.

Pharaoh's chief cupbearer, however, forgot all about Joseph, never giving him another thought. Two full years later, Pharaoh dreamed that he was standing on the bank of the Nile River. – Genesis 40:23, 41:1 (NLT)

But as for me, I watch in hope for the LORD, I wait for God my Savior; my God will hear me. – Micah 7:7

46

THE BOOMERANG OF ACTIONS

Give, and it will be given to you. A good measure, pressed down, shaken together and running over, will be poured into your lap. For with the measure you use, it will be measured to you. – Luke 6:38

Your actions, what you give and what you do will come back to you. Your actions and words are like a boomerang that you throw into the universe and, at the right time, they return. If you do good, good will come back to you. And if you choose to do wrong, your wrongdoing will also come back to you.

When King David and those remaining loyal to him fled the palace under cover of night because of his son Absalom's revolution, he didn't take any supplies with him. Old Barzillai, who had life experience, came to David in the desert with blankets, food, and all the necessities. After the revolt settled down, David called Barzillai on his way to the palace to tell him: "You did good for me, now is my turn to do something good for you. Come to the palace with me, and you will eat at my table. The good you did for me is coming back to you."

What you do will be done unto you is one of the principles of the Lord's kingdom. If you say a good word of encouragement, that good word will come back to you. You must use the blessings that the Lord gives you to be a blessing for others, and at the right time, these will come back to you and to your children.

If someone does you wrong, do not add another link to the evil chain of their wrongdoing; rather, repay the bad with good. Thus, you will stop the chain of wrongdoing from growing. Nothing in this world goes unrewarded. Do something good today, smile at someone, help someone in need and, at the right time, the boomerang of your actions will come back to you or to your children. Throw a boomerang of good into the universe today.

When you show mercy to the one who is in need, you will, in turn, receive mercy and grace when you go through a time of need. I, God, will send help to you in unexpected ways. Do not block the blessings that I give you by keeping them only to yourself but pass them on and the world will get better. This is a principle of My Kingdom. What you do, what you give, and how you judge will all come back to you. Do a good deed today or say a word that honors Me.

Cast your bread upon the waters, for you will find it after many days. – Ecclesiastes 11:1 (ESV)

Remember this: Whoever sows sparingly will also reap sparingly, and whoever sows generously will also reap generously. – 2 Corinthians 9:6

47

THE MEETING
ON THE SHORES OF FAILURE

He called out to them, "Friends, haven't you any fish?"
"No," they answered. He said, "Throw your net on the
right side of the boat and you will find some." When they
did, they were unable to haul the net in because of the
large number of fish. – John 21:5-6

The shore of failures is the place you reach when you realize that all of the efforts made were in vain and failed
to bring you any benefit. That is the moment when you realize
that you cannot continue in the same way. The shore of failures
is the place where Jesus likes to walk. He likes to meet people
going through the deep dark valleys of failure, bring them light,
and guide them. *"I am the Light of the world!"* He says.

The disciples were returning from a hard night of fishing.
Their nets were empty, and they were disappointed. Jesus told
them where they should cast their nets, and they caught an
abundance of fish. His word transformed the night of failure
into a morning of success.

Perhaps your nets are also empty in some aspects of life.
Your effort simply has not brought about any gain. I want to
remind you that God is the guide, He is the Light of the world,
and He is the One who will transform failure into success. He

knows where the schools of fish are located, so when you receive guidance from Him, your empty nets will be filled with blessings.

Many people meet regret, discouragement, and sorrow on the shores of failure. These three become their soul's road companions, and they don't want to speak to anyone else. However, Jesus wants to meet you regardless of your condition. He likes to walk through the valleys of failures and guide those who sit and talk with Him. Look and see how His footprints are by your side throughout these moments in your life.

My voice can whisper the solution to the crisis or pain you are experiencing. When you stay in My presence, I light up your dark valleys with My rays, and I will help you get out of them. The longer you stay in My presence, the easier it will be to avoid failures because I will guide you. Pray today for someone who is on the shore of failure and send a message. Do not let regret be your companion but make Me your travel partner instead.

Though he may stumble, he will not fall, for the LORD upholds him with his hand. – Psalm 37:24

But as for me, I watch in hope for the LORD, I wait for God my Savior; my God will hear me. Do not gloat over me, my enemy! Though I have fallen, I will rise. Though I sit in darkness, the LORD will be my light.
– Micah 7:7-8

48

THE ATMOSPHERE HAS INFLUENCE

When the priests withdrew from the Holy Place, the cloud filled the temple of the LORD. And the priests could not perform their service because of the cloud, for the glory of the LORD filled his temple. – 1 Kings 8:10-11

The atmosphere you are in will have an impact on your life. Whether or not you realize it, it will influence your spirit and soul. When you spend time in the Lord's presence, peace and joy will imperceptibly pour over you and strengthen you. You notice during prayer how His presence will descend over you in a heavenly way.

Just as mold and certain chemicals produce a toxic atmosphere, so do fear, panic and even people can produce a toxic spiritual atmosphere. When you open the door to your soul and let such a setting in, you will see how your emotions and actions will change, and you will feel sorrow.

The best antidote for a toxic spiritual atmosphere is time spent in the presence of the Lord. In those moments, peace begins to descend over you, and the promises of the Word give you courage and bravery to move forward. The presence of the Lord chases away the atmosphere of sin and brings a divine atmosphere of quiet, peace and joy that will uplift you. Sometimes you will probably be in the presence of the Lord, and no verse will resonate with your experience. My friend, do not get discouraged. By being in the atmosphere of His presence, you will breathe the clean air of heaven. Peace and joy will descend deep into your soul and chase out fear.

Young Samuel lived at the Temple, but some who resided there lived a life of sin. The atmosphere of sin was like a plague catching many in its net. Even though young Samuel lived there, he only opened the doors to his soul to the divine Words to take hold of his mind. Exposing himself to the presence of the Lord helped him surpass that toxic atmosphere haunted by sin and injustice. He carried the presence of the Lord wherever He went and, thus, the entire nation recognized he was the chosen one through whom God would work.

You will see that certain environments where you will find yourself will have a toxic atmosphere. In order to prevent this deadly environment from affecting you, you must spend time in the presence of the Lord to breathe the clean air of heaven. Even if you will feel that He is not speaking to you in a certain situation, the fact that you breathe the purified air of His presence will revitalize your soul. The atmosphere you are in will influence your life. Seek a pure atmosphere where He is present. He likes to work in an atmosphere of faith.

Spending quality time in My presence and allowing the pearls of My Word to enrich you spiritually will help you resist the pressing environment around you. What I want from you is that wherever you go, you change the atmosphere the way young Samuel did. As you hear My voice and stay in My presence, you will start to change the atmosphere without any words. I am with you, and

I will help you so that wherever there is tension, you can bring peace; wherever there is sorrow, you can bring joy; and wherever there is distrust, you can bring the confidence that comes from Me.

Whenever the spirit from God came on Saul, David would take up his lyre and play. Then relief would come to Saul; he would feel better, and the evil spirit would leave him. – 1 Samuel 16:23

You make known to me the path of life; you will fill me with joy in your presence, with eternal pleasures at your right hand. – Psalm 16:11

49

SIGNS OF GOODNESS

Even pull out some stalks for her from the bundles and leave them for her to pick up, and don't rebuke her. So Ruth gleaned in the field until evening. Then she threshed the barley she had gathered, and it amounted to about an ephah. – Ruth 2:16-17

God likes to sprinkle signs of His goodness in your path. When you go through difficult times, it will be easier to notice them and understand them because those signs will mean much to you. The signs of goodness are the gifts that He places along your road to remind you that He loves you.

Ruth was experiencing a difficult time. She was gathering up the wheat of the poor to make a loaf of bread for herself and her mother-in-law. But God opened the heart of the landowner to her, and he told his servants to leave extra wheat in her path. On that day, she gathered up a small bag filled with barley, which was a wonder for their situation. Little did Ruth realize that the bag of barley was the sign of divine goodness toward her.

When you will see the signs of divine goodness toward you—whether at your job, in your finances, or in other aspects, you should thank God. Your gratitude is the language of your love toward Him, which increases the faith you have in Him.

Remember: you are also obligated to sprinkle signs of goodness to others around you. If someone will try to thank you for what you have done for them, accept the thanks. Do not forget to direct their gaze to God's goodness. What you do today will come back to you in the future.

In your past, you have seen how My goodness has been manifested toward you. You have seen the signs of My goodness that I have left along your path. To be like Me, you will have to do the same. This week, sprinkle a sign of divine goodness in someone's path, do a favor, help, bless, and do something specific to direct people's gaze toward Me. Do those deeds without expecting anything back. The reward is from Me.

I remain confident of this: I will see the goodness of the LORD *in the land of the living. Wait for the* LORD; *be strong and take heart and wait for the* LORD.
– Psalm 27:13-14

And God is able to bless you abundantly, so that in all things at all times, having all that you need, you will abound in every good work.
– 2 Corinthians 9:8

50

A FAVORABLE WIND

God's mighty power sent a strong wind from the southeast, and it brought birds that covered the ground, like sand on the beach. Then God made the birds fall in the camp of his people near their tents. – Psalm 78:26-28 (CEV)

Oftentimes, life can be compared to a boat trip. Along the sea of life, some waves will rise menacingly, or storms will buffet your life's ship. Perhaps you have also experienced moments when you wanted to move ahead in a certain direction, and no matter how much you rowed with all of your might, the progress was insignificant. The wind was seemingly against you. Perhaps at other times whether you were in your own life's boat or accompanying others, you saw how God miraculously caused a favorable wind to blow and move the ship ahead.

The Hebrew people were in the desert without resources, but God caused a strong wind to blow, thereby providing the food they needed to come to their tent doors. He can just as easily cause winds of blessings to blow over your life!

Perhaps now you are struggling to progress in a certain area, and you have used up all of the resources you had with insignificant results. Sometimes the Lord wants to bring you to a point where you see that the blessing comes from Him as opposed to being the product of your effort. He wants to send a favorable wind to blow in the sails of your life's boat and bring you to the blessed lands He has prepared for you. The favor that you will gain among people who can open doors of opportunities, He wants you to tie them to His goodness. When the LORD unleashes a favorable wind in the spiritual atmosphere, it takes effect in the material and relational realms, as well as in other aspects of life.

Resist the doubts knocking at your mind's door, trying to convince you that nothing good will happen to you. Pray for the blessings of heaven and earth to come over your life and your family. Thank Him for the favorable wind that will blow His blessings your way.

What I want to teach you is that beyond your efforts, there is divine favor. I can send a favorable wind over your finances, I can open blessed doors for you, and I can surprise you in different ways with what I will do for you. When you understand the grace and favor that I have prepared for you to be fresh each day, you will start your day with joy and enthusiasm, waiting to see how I will surprise you. Step forward on this day with confidence for I will send a favorable wind to your ship's sails to lead them to blessed lands and restful waters. I am by your side.

Then Moses stretched out his hand over the sea, and all that night the LORD drove the sea back with a strong

east wind and turned it into dry land. The waters were divided, and the Israelites went through the sea on dry ground, with a wall of water on their right and on their left. – Exodus 14:21

He lays the beams of his chambers on the waters; he makes the clouds his chariot; he rides on the wings of the wind; he makes his messengers winds, his ministers a flaming fire. – Psalm 104:3-4 (ESV)

51

THE WATCHMAN

I will stand at my watch and station myself on the ramparts; I will look to see what he will say to me, and what answer I am to give to this complaint. – Habakkuk 2:1

When you spend time in the presence of the LORD in prayer and meditation, you are climbing the "watchtower." From that vantage point, you will easily be able to see what is approaching your life's citadel.

In olden times, the role of the watchman was to stand in the tower and look toward the horizon to watch for the approach of a foreign army or any danger. Those who stood watch in the tower could see far in the distance and were responsible to report what they observed on the horizon to prepare the citadel inhabitants.

When Habakkuk climbed his "watchtower," he was going to prayer, seeking the face of God. In His watchtower, he would find what the Lord said would happen in the near future and how He would answer his questions. In the same way, when you spend time with the Lord, you are actually climbing the watchtower and listening to the Lord's message that will prepare you for each day ahead. This time is precious because He will strengthen you and provide you with divine guidance and revelation. Do not consider that time as being wasted or fruitless because the Lord may speak to you about matters that your human eyes cannot see and that you cannot anticipate through intelligence. His presence will bring you revelation and light about what you must tell others and the moments when you will must remain silent. When you stay in the presence of the Lord, you will receive specific promises for your life that you will have to take note of and keep your sight on until they are fulfilled.

I want to speak to you and reveal My plans to you. The promises I will tell you will be fulfilled at the right time, but you must wait in faith. When you stay and talk with Me, I will prepare you for what you have to face on this day. I will light up certain verses of My Word and, when the time is right, you will understand and apply them. My Spirit and My Word work together. Step forward on this day with confidence that I am by your side.

Son of man, I have made you a watchman for the people of Israel; so hear the word I speak and give them warning from me. – Ezekiel 3:17

I wait for the Lord, my whole being waits, and in his word I put my hope. I wait for the Lord more than watchmen wait for the morning, more than watchmen wait for the morning. Israel, put your hope in the Lord, for with the Lord is unfailing love and with him is full redemption. – Psalm 130:5-7

52

TAKE THE FIRST STEP, AND I WILL SHOW YOU THE SECOND ONE

The LORD had said to Abram, "Go from your country, your people and your father's household to the land I will show you. – Genesis 12:1 (NLT)

God will not reveal the complete details of His plan for your life all at one time. Once you take the first step, He will reveal the second, and so on. His desire is to increase your faith and reliance on Him.

When you listen to the Lord's voice and take steps in the direction in which He guides you, those around you will not understand. You will not know all of the steps you have to take or how the finished product will look or even the product that results from divine guidance. You will be misunderstood and misjudged because whoever thinks in the earthly realm will want to know the details, direction and the end result from the very beginning. The godly man—that man of faith who listens and takes steps guided by the Lord cannot explain all of the details to the natural man. After all, the godly man does not yet know them, but because he is certain that God's plan will be blessed, he will take step after step in the direction that He indicates.

Abraham received the promise of a land that would belong

to him and his descendants. He received guidance for the first step, but the exact details of the journey were unknown to him. How embarrassed might Abraham have felt if someone close to him would have asked him for details about the direction he would travel, exactly where he would settle, and how certain he was about that place.

When you take the step of obeying the Lord, you will not know each step of what you will have to do. Revelation and fulfilment of His plans for your life are closely tied to each step of your obedience. He wants you to stay in close contact with Him to understand the direction and the next step. The trap into which many fall is enthusiastically running ahead before the Lord can reveal the next step of His plan. Stay in close touch with Him, and He will tell you how to take the next step and in what direction so that you do not make mistakes.

When you hear My voice and the steps I ask you to take, you must not let the doubt sowed by others defeat you. Their words of disapproval must make you seek Me even more. With every step you take in the direction I indicate to you, your faith will grow even more and you will be more certain. I will surround you with people who will support you in what you have to do. Develop a keen ear for My voice and step with certainty. After some time, you will look back and be amazed of what you were able to accomplish with Me. With every step you take obeying Me, you will be more and more comfortable walking by faith.

By faith Abraham, when called to go to a place he
would later receive as his inheritance, obeyed and went,
even though he did not know where he was going.
– Hebrew 11:8

Whether you turn to the right or to the left, your ears
will hear a voice behind you, saying,
"This is the way; walk in it." – Isaiah 30:21

53

LIFE IS MADE UP OF DIFFERENT CHAPTERS

For everything there is a season, a time for every activity under heaven. A time to be born and a time to die. A time to plant and a time to harvest. A time to cry and a time to laugh. A time to grieve and a time to dance. – Ecclesiastes 3:1-2, 4 (NLT)

Life is like a book composed of multiple chapters. Some chapters will be filled with light, joy and enthusiasm, and others will detail sorrow, mistakes and sadness. Just as it is not good to judge a book after a single chapter or based on the cover, it is not good to judge your life or others' lives by a single event or a single chapter.

Solomon speaks of a season of joy and of tears, a season for planting and then harvesting, of life and of death, and of many others in life. The Bible also contains many chapters with which we can identify. Sometimes we might be in the chapter of tears with the prophet Jeremiah. Other times, we might be in the chapter of victory with David. We might be in the chapter of betrayal like Jesus, or we might be in the chapter of joy like Abraham when God fulfilled His promise of a son to him. In each season you experience, you must be certain that you are protected under the wings of the Most High and that He is by your side.

Many fall into the trap of believing that life is entirely made up of the atmosphere of a single chapter. Some believe that the tears won't end, and others believe that the joy is unending. Whatever situation you are facing, you must pass through it alongside God. When you are in the frozen winter season and you see no way ahead in the blizzard, remember that He is the Sun of Righteousness from whom you can receive spiritual warmth. In the winter of life is the time when visions are born and grow as the spring of activities approaches. When you are in the season of harvest and are enjoying the fruit of your labor, thank Him because all things come from Him. The Lord works in your life in each chapter—even if He sometimes works behind the scenes.

I will be by your side at all times. Before you were born, I saw where you would go. I saw your joy and your sadness. Stay by Me, and you will understand much of what is happening to you. Stay by Me, and I will guide you through the hard times so I can share your resulting joy with Me. I want you to reach maturity and understand that, even in the soul's moments of winter, I will walk by your side. That is the stage of faith I want you to embrace.

Your eyes saw my unformed body; all the days ordained for me were written in your book before one of them came to be. – Psalm 139:16

As you do not know the path of the wind, or how the body is formed in a mother's womb, so you cannot understand the work of God, the Maker of all things.
– Ecclesiastes 11:5

That person is like a tree planted by streams of water, which yields its fruit in season and whose leaf does not wither—whatever they do prospers.
– Psalm 1:3

54

FREE THE PRISONERS

Perhaps the reason he was separated from you for a little while was that you might have him back forever—no longer as a slave, but better than a slave, as a dear brother. He is very dear to me but even dearer to you, both as a fellow man and as a brother in the Lord. – Philemon 1:15-16

Man tends to label others based on what they have done and then holds them prisoners to those labels. When someone has wronged you and hurt you, the natural tendency is to categorize that person based on what was done. That person is the thief, the arrogant one—the sinner. Even if the person admitted the mistake and asked forgiveness, you still tend to keep him or her as the prisoner of past mistakes. However, if the Lord has freed you from your past of mistakes and sins, and He sees you as pure through Jesus Christ, shouldn't you also free people from the labels you have assigned them?

Onesimus, Philemon's slave, one day stole his master's money and ran away. After some time, young Onesimus met the apostle Paul, repented of his former deeds, started to follow the Lord and returned to Philemon to ask for forgiveness.

In his letter mediating for Onesimus, the apostle Paul told Philemon that he would pay for the damages caused by the young slave. He also mentioned an important detail: *"receive*

Onesimus now as a beloved brother." Forgiving his runaway slave and looking at him as a beloved brother was not easy for Philemon, but he did as God had done for him. Likewise, God has forgiven your mistakes of the past and sees you as blameless through the Lord Jesus.

If you have people in your life who have done you wrong and have corrected their ways, you need to change their labels and your attitude toward them. When you free people in your heart, you will gain freedom at the spiritual level. If God forgave you and no longer holds you responsible for the past, shouldn't you do the same for others?

What I want from you is to free the people you hold prisoner in your heart. Yes, I understand they have wronged you and have treated you unjustly, but your heart must be filled with My presence—not filled with the files of mistakes made by others. When you forgive and allow My presence fully into your heart, then joy and peace will fill more of your heart. You will live differently as you undo some chains, break some chains, rip up labels and show someone who is perhaps undeserving that you are like Me and you possess My character.

The Spirit of the Sovereign Lord is on me, because the Lord has anointed me to proclaim good news to the poor. He has sent me to bind up the brokenhearted, to proclaim freedom for the captives and release from darkness for the prisoners... – Isaiah 61:1

You will open the eyes of the blind. You will free the captives from prison, releasing those who sit in dark dungeons. – Isaiah 42:7 (NLT)

55

THE LENSES YOU LOOK THROUGH

But because my servant Caleb has a different spirit and follows me wholeheartedly, I will bring him into the land he went to, and his descendants will inherit it. – Numbers 14:24

Your attitude before life's challenges will be influenced by the lenses through which you look. If you look through the lens of fear and powerlessness, you will take a step back when facing problems. You will feel inadequate facing these complications. If you look through the filter of faith, you know God is by your side; He is your support and shelter. Then you will advance with confidence and courage.

After scouting the Promised Land, the twelve men returned to Moses. They all brought the same report: "that it was a rich country and that giants lived there." However, when they started to share information about their ability to defeat the giants, the twelve spies sharply parted into two divisions. Ten men interpreted it through the lens of fear, seeing themselves as mere grasshoppers against the giants. However, Joshua and Caleb interpreted the nation's conquering ability through the lens of faith—God was on their side, and they could defeat the challenges and the giants.

In life, you will interpret problems through the filters you develop daily. If you allow faith and trust in God to grow, you will advance with daring steps toward life's problems. If you allow fear to reign in your mind, you will retreat. During this time in your life, work on the filters or lenses through which you see the problems and complications of life. Make sure the lenses are characterized by faith and always be led by the Lord's Spirit. His Word will help you develop the lenses of faith and move ahead with confidence.

I am on your side. I have supported you thus far and will continue to be your shield. Analyze each problem that comes along your path, knowing that I am Almighty, and I am your support. As you grow increasingly greater faith in Me each day, your courage will grow. Rely on the promises of My Word and learn from the experiences that I have designed to teach you about faith. When you step daringly, knowing that I am with you, that attitude will pass on courage to those near you. Displaying the boldness I give you is one way you can confess Me before others.

Finally, be strong in the Lord and in his mighty power.
– Ephesians 6:10

So do not fear, for I am with you; do not be dismayed, for I am your God. I will strengthen you and help you; I will uphold you with my righteous right hand.
– Isaiah 41:10

56

MOUNTAINS AND VALLEYS

About eight days after Jesus said this, he took Peter, John and James with him and went up onto a mountain to pray. As he was praying, the appearance of his face changed, and his clothes became as bright as a flash of lightning.... The next day, when they came down from the mountain, a large crowd met him. A man in the crowd called out, "Teacher, I beg you to look at my son, for he is my only child." – Luke 9:28-29, 37-38.

Life goes between these two extremes: the mountain of divine presence and the valley of despair. When you are on the mountain in the presence of the Lord, your soul fills with joy, power and light. The mountain is the place where you wish to be permanently. However, life is also composed of the valleys. When you leave the heights of the mountain to descend into the dark valleys of pain, you must bring the divine presence, power and light to cross the crevasse of sorrow. People in the valley also need the bright light received by the person standing on the mountain in the presence of the Almighty.

Jesus was on the mountain of Transfiguration, and while He prayed, His face was transformed. He received power and conversed with Moses and Elijah for strength. When He descended into the valley, He encountered the pain of a father who needed the healing power of the One who had stood in prayer in the presence of the Father. The disciples who did not climb the mountain struggled to free the possessed boy but were unable to unchain him.

During the time you spend in the presence of the Lord, you will be filled with brightness. This spiritual brilliance will be noticed by those around you who are walking in darkness. On the mountain is where He prepares you to lift up the sorrows you will encounter in the valley of pain. Transform the valley of despair into the atmosphere you felt on the mountain of divine presence. Certainly, you will meet people who will need encouragement and the power you received on the mountain in His presence.

What I want from you in this time when you seek Me is to allow your soul to be taken over by power, brilliance, joy and guidance. You will use these blessings in the valleys that you will go through, but they will also be used to lift others from their despair. Thus, you will advance My kingdom in the dark valleys that you will cross.

When Moses came down from Mount Sinai with the two tablets of the covenant law in his hands, he was not aware that his face was radiant because he had spoken with the LORD. – Exodus 34:29

When they walk through the Valley of Weeping, it will become a place of refreshing springs. The autumn rains will clothe it with blessings. – Psalm 84:6 (NLT)

57

SIGNS OF ENCOURAGEMENT

Look at the birds of the air; they do not sow or reap or store away in barns, and yet your heavenly Father feeds them. Are you not much more valuable than they? – Matthew 6:26

Each person needs encouragement for the hard times but also for the good times in life. Encouragement is like the wind flowing under a bird's wings elevating its flight. God has lovingly placed different signs around you to remind you of His promises. Sometimes, certain people will be an encouragement for you. Other times, flowers, mementoes, or animals will be His indicators to direct your thoughts to divine promises. Encouragement is for the soul what oxygen is for the body.

When you see the birds of the sky who haven't collected any food for the winter ahead, be reminded that the LORD who cares for them will also care for you. He is your Father, and He will lead you to green pastures and restful waters.

When you see the beauty of flowers and how they are dressed, remember that they do not buy clothes, but God dresses them in a wonderful way. Likewise, He will also provide what you need.

When you see lion cubs going to bed hungry, remember His promise that *"those who seek the Lord do not lack anything."*

Signs of encouragement are indicators along your life's road to remind you about His care. When worry and sorrow, the Evil One's agents, prey upon your mind's chamber, the promises of His Word will expel them. His Words are like rays of light that penetrate beyond the curtain of worry casting a shade on the joy of the soul and making the light of His presence chase away sorrows.

I wish for My Spirit to connect the signs I have left in your path with My promises daily. You must be attentive and watchful to see the signs I have sprinkled on your road, and you must get used to hearing My whisper. My child, encourage a sorrowful soul today. Make the rays of My promises penetrate a soul that is pressed down by worry. If you want to be like Me, you must also put signs of encouragement in the paths of those who are dejected, causing the one who finds them look toward Me."

The lions may grow weak and hungry, but those who seek the LORD *lack no good thing.* – Psalm 34:10

And these are but the outer fringe of his works; how faint the whisper we hear of him! Who then can understand the thunder of his power? – Job 26:14

His splendor was like the sunrise; rays flashed from his hand, where his power was hidden. – Habakkuk 3:4

58

ADVANCEMENT

But thanks be to God, who in Christ always leads us in triumphal procession, and through us spreads the fragrance of the knowledge of him everywhere. – 2 Corinthians 2:14 (ESV)

The Lord's plan for you is advancement. Each day, you must advance along the road you are walking—from Calvary to heavenly glory. The Lord has prepared for you His chariot of victory in which you will take this journey. The more you obey the One who leads the chariot of victory, the more you will have an ample view of the direction in which you are going and what He wants you to do.

For some, the trip in the victory chariot seems boring, and they become disenchanted because they have not connected with the Lord's vision. Others do not like the journey because they allow themselves to be courted by sinful passions and stop at various tempting and promising rest stops. Later, they realize that they have fallen into the trap of their earthly nature and feel a great deal of sorrow. My child, cut the ropes of carelessness and sin that try to slyly tie you in their snares to prevent your advancing.

Look and let yourself be encouraged by the great cloud of witnesses, by the heroes of faith the holy Book mentions, and by those who have defeated sorrows and challenges and have arrived at their destinations victorious.

When you stay in My presence, the veils blocking your understanding of the work I do in the world start to be cast aside. The more you understand the direction and the waves that I stir, the more enthusiasm will begin to take over you. Refuse the shining attractions of the earthly realm that leave a bitter taste in your mouth for a long time and place veils over your spiritual eyes. Stay in the light of My Word, and I will show you My plans for you.

With your help I can advance against a troop; with my God I can scale a wall. – Psalm 18:29

Then the LORD will appear over them; his arrow will flash like lightning. The Sovereign LORD will sound the trumpet; he will march in the storms of the south…
– Zechariah 9:14

59

BROADEN YOUR BORDERS

Enlarge the place of your tent, stretch your tent curtains wide, do not hold back; lengthen your cords, strengthen your stakes. – Isaiah 54:2

This period in your life must be a time when you expand your territories. Your talents, family, spiritual gifts, material possessions, influence, the job you have, and many other benefits are the territories that God has entrusted to you. These territories are like a tent that must be extended. God's plan is for you to broaden your borders and horizons. The Evil One's plan is to set obstacles that block you. Some limitations were placed on you by other people who told you that you can't accomplish more. Those words limited your life's territories. Other limitations are placed in your life by fear, the lack of faith, the lack of confidence or vision, and many others.

The Parable of the Talents tells how the Lord gave each person gold talents and how each one was responsible for developing, expanding and multiplying their talents. The Lord condemned limitation. With each territory you conquer, you realize that you can do more. When you conquer a territory, you realize that you do not want to restrict yourself but find additional courage to advance. When you conquer certain territories, you will realize that some are in a drought, and you will have to take the Water of Life to those lands. The kingdom of God must progress and must develop, and you are His ambassador on this earth.

I have blessed you with various talents, material possessions, and influence. I want you to develop these gifts I have given you and put them into My service. Through them, I work to develop My kingdom. You are My representative here, and I am with you and want you to develop as much as possible. Do not limit yourself because I have placed immense capability within you. When the Evil One tries to steal a territory from you, fight back to regain it. Use as much of the capabilities you have to develop My kingdom."

You enlarged my path under me, So my feet did not slip.
– Psalm 18:36 (NKJV)

Jabez cried out to the God of Israel, "Oh, that you would bless me and enlarge my territory! Let your hand be with me and keep me from harm so that I will be free from pain." And God granted his request.
– 1 Chronicles 4:10

60

LOSSES AND GAINS

For I know the plans I have for you," declares the LORD, *"plans to prosper you and not to harm you, plans to give you hope and a future. –* Jeremiah 29:11

No one likes to lose; but loss is one of the means that God uses to redirect your life or to give you something better. Do not be upset if you have suffered loss because God allowed it for a purpose. Each painful trial or test coming your way has first gone through His hand as a designer, and He has molded the type and intensity of the challenge.

Saul searched for his father's lost donkeys that represented his family's business. Losing valuable essentials for the family business is no easy loss to absorb. However, God orchestrated that loss for a short time, so that in the course of Saul's search he would cross the path of the prophet Samuel, who would anoint Saul to become the first king of Israel. After that divine appointment, his father's donkeys were found.

God works in mysterious ways—always for your good. If you have lost something in life, know that God allowed your loss for a specific purpose. He occasionally uses this method to redirect you to His plans. Sometimes what you already have in your hands and what you care about with all your soul does not include His plans, and He wants to give you something better.

The tears you spill when you lose must be shed before Him and wiped with the handkerchief of trust in Him. He has a better plan—even if you cannot understand. Loss can require a decisive step of faith.

Even if right now you don't understand why certain things have been taken from your hands, I want to remind you that I am a good Father who cares about you, and I will change your tears into joy at the right time. I have prepared gifts to bring you spiritual joy. Until then, you have to walk by faith and wait. All things are working together for your good. Thank Me through faith because I will change your disadvantage to an advantage and will turn the situation in your favor. All things work together for your good.

As for the donkeys you lost three days ago, do not worry about them; they have been found. And to whom is all the desire of Israel turned, if not to you and your whole family line? – 1 Samuel 9:20

I will give you back what you lost in the years when swarms of locusts ate your crops. It was I who sent this army against you. – Joel 2:25 (GNT)

61

THE LESSON OF LEFTOVERS

Don't you understand even yet? Don't you remember the 5,000 I fed with five loaves, and the baskets of leftovers you picked up? – Matthew 16:9 (NLT)

When you experience victory, may I remind you that the Lord gives you different souvenirs to take with you into the next episode of life's challenges. After Jesus multiplied the bread and fishes for the five thousand people and fed them, He told the disciples to gather up all of the leftovers. The disciples then boarded a ship to go to the other side. A severe storm suddenly set in that endangered the boat's occupants, causing the disciples to fear for their lives. The black clouds of despair descended upon them—exactly as they just as they plummet down on many people today.

The baskets filled with pieces of bread and fish carried with them on the ship were the irrefutable evidence of the miracle that Jesus had performed only hours early. These remnants were a strong and unquestionable testimony that God possessed the power to calm the crisis in which they now found themselves. Likewise, in your life, you will need to gather as much testimony of divine intervention as possible from your experiences. These evidences will be useful to you when you need to move forward in life's tumultuous moments. If you don't take note of the Holy Spirit's messages resonating power-fully in your soul, they will be forgotten and covered by other voices making room for themselves to be heard much louder. If you do not write about the divine imprints in the fabric of the events of your life, they will soon be forgotten, and other dramatic events will take their place.

What is your basket of bread and fish? What are the souve-nirs you took with you from past experiences? What are the di-vine messages and marks that you keep with care? Show God's fingerprints on your past to a friend who is going through some difficult storms and thus give him the wings of faith to rise up beyond the storm clouds surrounding his life. Your life's story must be a testimony of victory throughout the experi-ences you've had.

Every victory that you will have alongside Me will have to create a testimony—a mark or a souvenir to re-mind you of My power when you go through your next challenge. These evidences prove that I can help you get through the rising storm. I will be with you. Be like a merchant, knowing how to put in and take out new and old things and from your life's storeroom that speak of My interventions. These testimonies or souvenirs will help you and will help those close to you go forward through life's most difficult moments.

When they had all had enough to eat, he said to his dis-ciples, "Gather the pieces that are left over. Let nothing be wasted." – John 6:12

When you pass through the waters, I will be with you;
and when you pass through the rivers, they will not
sweep over you. When you walk through the fire, you
will not be burned; the flames will not set you ablaze.
– Isaiah 43:2

So do not fear, for I am with you; do not be dismayed,
for I am your God. I will strengthen you and help you;
I will uphold you with my righteous right hand.
– Isaiah 41:10

62

CHASING AWAY FEAR

*For God has said, "I will never fail you. I will never aban-
don you." So, we can say with confidence, "The Lord is
my helper, so I will have no fear. What can mere people
do to me?"* – Hebrew 13:5-6

God's power is the greatest in the universe. He is on your
side and will support you on this day as well. Fear is an
unseen plague that grips many souls in its claws. Many people
who start their day with a heavy soul do not realize the heaviness is because of fear that has erupted in their life. Staying in
the presence of the Lord chases out this thief of joy and hope.
Feeling fear is normal, but sorrow, enchainment, and the effects
produced by fear are not normal for a child of God.

The way to cast away fear from your life is to obey and inter-
nalize His promises to you. Your soul must absorb these promises the same way dry soil absorbs water, and these promises
must touch each fiber of your soul. You must proclaim them in
your life and bathe your mind in them. One of His promises is:
the Lord is on your side and will support you every day of your
life. When you absorb His promises in your mind, the tentacles
of fear are severed and cast away from your life. When you feel
His breath in your ears and see His shadow on your hand, you
begin to move forward with confidence. The Lord's Word gives

you the courage of a lion to move forward and meet the day that you are facing.

What is your fear? What is your sorrow? Confront them with His promises: "I will never leave you nor forsake you." "You are my beloved." "I will guide you." "I will bless you."

Where the love of God lives in the heart, fear has no place and is cast away by the warm and bright rays of divine presence, which chase out any shadow of doubt. Do not let thoughts and feelings of sorrow set into your life; rather, confront them with His promises and His love.

The more My presence lives in you, the more fear and doubt will disappear. When your mind and soul absorb My promises, then confidence, courage and faith begin to bloom in your heart. The scent of these divine flowers will change the atmosphere around you. Walking through faith will bring divine intangibles into your home and in those around you. This is one of the ways you can relight the flame of faith and courage in the lives of others.

His splendor was like the sunrise; rays flashed from his hand, where his power was hidden. – Habakkuk 3:4

There is no fear in love. But perfect love drives out fear, because fear has to do with punishment. The one who fears is not made perfect in love. – 1 John 4:18

The Spirit you received does not make you slaves, so

that you live in fear again; rather, the Spirit you received brought about your adoption to sonship. And by him we cry, "Abba, Father." – Romans 8:15

63

Rest in My Presence

Even youths grow tired and weary, and young men stumble and fall; but those who hope in the Lord will renew their strength. They will soar on wings like eagles; they will run and not grow weary, they will walk and not be faint. – Isaiah 40:30-31

The daily rush, repetitive work, stress and pressures often tire the soul and the body. Sometimes the blows that a weary person suffers cause him to retreat to the cave of loneliness and discouragement.

The prophet Elijah was a man of faith, but the weariness and threats caused him to embrace hopelessness. He ran away and retreated to a cave far away from the others and far from his God-given ministry. He took refuge in the cave of loneliness and disappointment.

When God passed by the cave entrance, He gently whispered, "What are you doing here, Elijah?"

When God looks at you, He often sees you withdrawn into assorted caves where your soul takes refuge from various disappointments and fatigue. He approaches you and asks you in a gentle voice, "What are you doing in a state such as this? My child, you can achieve a rest for the soul when you stay in His presence, and you must seek this rest daily."

Even if the waves rise and many matters shake your soul, do not forget that He is in control. He wants to pour a drop of His divine peace into your soul, making you like a lighthouse facing a stormy sea. The rest you will feel in His presence will increase your faith and melt your discouragement.

When you take a step in His presence, you leave the crazy rush of the world's storm and put your faith in Him. You declare that He alone has the helm of your life, and He will lead you to restful waters. Do not depend on outside circumstances to bring you peace because life is like a small boat in the middle of an ocean's waves. Instead depend on God alone who will give your ship direction. When I have Him on my righthand side, I do not falter.

Even if weariness has overtaken you; I want to remind you that I can revive you. When you spend time in My presence reading My words and placing your sorrows in My hands, you will start to gain power and clarity over the situations you are experiencing. You are my beloved child, and I have an outstanding plan for you. I would like you to rest in My presence to allow your mind to consume My Word. Thus, you will see how I will carry your life's boat above the waves toward restful waters.

Come to me, all you who are weary and burdened, and I will give you rest. – Matthew 11:28

When Elijah heard it, he pulled his cloak over his face

and went out and stood at the mouth of the cave. Then a voice said to him, "What are you doing here, Elijah?" He replied, "I have been very zealous for the LORD God Almighty." – 1 Kings 19:13

I will refresh the weary and satisfy the faint."
– Jeremiah 31:25

64

Examine Your Life

Let us examine our ways and test them and let us return to the Lord. – Lamentations 3:40

Examine any concerns, attitudes, and people entering your life under the light of the Word. Your life is similar to an old citadel enclosed by walls, which must be guarded. Within the citadel of your life, various people and spiritual states often enter and influence your direction and future. You must, therefore, examine under the light of the Word what you will allow to enter and stay within your citadel's walls.

A disobedient man full of bad thoughts once entered one of the Hebrew citadels of the Old Testament. He hid among the crowd so that no one would see him. King David's general tracked him down with his army, and reaching the citadel where he hid, the general wanted to assail the citadel's walls to capture the man. The general was ready to deal considerable damage to the citadel, but a wise woman who understood the gravity of the situation spoke to the leaders to remove the problematic man from their midst. She convinced them to look for the intruder and hand him over to the general so that their place would not be destroyed by the king's armies.

In the citadel of your life, various people, ideas, and attitudes will enter unfelt. Some will be good influences and will be great blessings for you; however, others will bring a negative influence through their presence. You must sometimes stop and check each person, item, idea or attitude that enters your mind's citadel. Performing this analysis under the light of the holy Word will reveal to you what you must accept and prize and what you must change in order to lead a fulfilled life.

The assessment of your life that I am calling you to make will help you to grow spiritually and will make joy be part of your life. Put people, attitudes and spiritual states coming into your life under My light. Some will be a great blessing for you, and others will bring you great loss over time. You need the discernment that comes under the light of My presence. I want your life to be lived abundantly and any attempt to defraud it by different spirits or negative attitudes can be revealed in My presence.

But everything exposed by the light becomes visible--and everything that is illuminated becomes a light.
– Ephesians 5:13

Everyone who does evil hates the light and will not come into the light for fear that their deeds will be exposed. But whoever lives by the truth comes into the light, so that it may be seen plainly that what they have done has been done in the sight of God. – John 3:20-21

Examine yourselves to see whether you are in the faith; test yourselves. Do you not realize that Christ Jesus is in you— unless, of course, you fail the test? – 2 Corinthians 13:5

65

A New Identity

Therefore, if anyone is in Christ, the new creation has come: The old has gone, the new is here! – 2 Corinthians 5:17

One of your greatest battles will be coming to the point of seeing yourself as God sees you. Many sorrows will be removed from your life when you understand your position in Christ, i.e., "you are a new creation." The way in which you see yourself is closely connected to the thoughts ruminating in your mind and what you allow to define you. Some people have allowed themselves to be defined by material possessions or by their successes, and once these tangibles disappeared, they were left in a desolate state. Others plummeted so deep into their pain that their lives were defined by their hopelessness.

Naomi went through various episodes of drama, pain and suffering that profoundly marked her life, influencing her identity. Although her name, *Naomi* meant "pleasant," she asked her friends and neighbors to call her *Mara*, meaning "sorrow" because life had given her many bitter pills. She began to see herself through the prism of her pain, allowing it to define her identity. However, God never called her under this name because He saw her value, as He also sees our value beyond the sorrows that we experience.

Look at your life through the prism of what God says about you. Consider yourself as He sees you. Do not allow your problems, wounds and failures to define you. You cannot ruminate on thoughts of victimization while also living victoriously. You must let the power of the Word to trace the image of victory alongside Him in your life. On the other hand, do not allow yourself to be defined by the euphoric successes that deceive many. Proclaim your position in Christ over your life and look at yourself as He sees you. You are His beloved child. You are a new being, the old is gone. You are forgiven of all sins through Jesus. You are saved, and you are more than victorious through Him.

Many forces and ideas will try to create a new identity for you, including the world, people, and new ideologies. Throughout all of these ideological waves that arise, you will need to stand tall and proclaim that you are My beloved child. My opinion about you is the most important. Anchor yourself to My Word and seek to understand the position in which I have placed you in Christ to live a victorious life. I love you with an eternal love; you are Mine.

Instead, let the Spirit renew your thoughts and attitudes. Put on your new nature, created to be like God— truly righteous and holy. – Ephesians 3:23-24 (NLT)

The LORD appeared to us in the past, saying: "I have loved you with an everlasting love; I have drawn you with unfailing kindness. – Jeremiah 31:3

66

STIRRING THE NEST

Like an eagle that stirs up its nest, that flutters over its young, spreading out its wings, catching them, bearing them on its pinions, the LORD alone guided him, no foreign god was with him. – Deuteronomy 32:11-12 (ESV)

One of the methods that God uses in life is to stir the nest like an eagle. When He has planned to make a change in a person's life, He applies this method. Stirring the nest is painful because the process brings a hurtful break from the past, but its purpose is to bring about development, blessing and fulfillment of destiny.

The mother eagle prepares a comfortable nest for its chicks and feeds them well. However, after the eagle chicks grow to young adulthood, the mother begins to stir their comfortable nest, making it unpleasant for them to stay. Perhaps she even resorts to pushing them from the nest to teach them how to fly. She knows what is appropriate for the young chicks. The nest is comfortable, but eagles are not meant to spend their lives within the confines of a pleasant nest. They are meant to explore the sky, search the horizon, and wander the world. The chicks are created for something more than simply sitting in the nest and having their needs met.

When the Lord created you, He instilled certain qualities

and untold potential within you. His employing this method of stirring your comfortable nest is to help you start flapping your wings and flying. He wants you to develop the qualities and potential lying dormant within you. The purpose is for you to ascend to the next level, expand your territories and pursue your potential.

Stirring your life's nest means pain and discomfort, but you will grow through this means. When the Lord uses this method, do not oppose Him; rather, acquiesce so that you may understand the direction in which He wants to take you. When you listen to Him closely—even if you felt pain and you don't understand, the answers that will be in your favor will eventually be revealed. When life closes a door, don't forget that the Lord will open a blessed gate because He wants what is best for you. The Lord is like a great eagle who has carried you on His wings, has led you and has pushed you outside of your comfortable nest to fulfill your destiny.

When someone is not attentive or afraid to take the next step, I apply this method of stirring the nest. I know what qualities I have placed in you that you are not employing. I know better what you can do and what you can accomplish, and the fact that you have retreated into the comfortable nest with all the talents that I have placed in you is like a waste in My eyes. Be attentive when He encourages you to spread your wings and fly to new territories. If you work with Me, you will see how far you will go.

You yourselves have seen what I did to Egypt, and how I carried you on eagles' wings and brought you to myself.
– Exodus 19:4

I will be your God throughout your lifetime—until your hair is white with age. I made you, and I will care for you. I will carry you along and save you.
– Isaiah 46:4 (NLT)

67

THE COURAGE TO MOVE FORWARD

Be strong and very courageous. Be careful to obey all the law my servant Moses gave you; do not turn from it to the right or to the left, that you may be successful wherever you go. – Joshua 1:7

Your courage must be fueled by the time spent in the presence of the Lord. When you rely only on your abilities and resources, you will notice that they are insufficient when facing certain crises, and your courage will be paralyzed. If you rely on God who is the Alpha and the Omega, the Beginning and the End, the Almighty One, you will see the roots of your courage draw its nutrients from the power of His presence.

This day has its challenges, but your courage will be great when you rely on Him, who is your strength, your shelter and your hope. In the work that He has entrusted to you, you will sometimes feel like you are inadequate or like you're skating in place. That is the moment when you must get closer to Him and recharge your energy from His power.

Moses received the mission to go before the Pharaoh to free God's people. He saw himself as insignificant and inadequate for such a work. However, the Lord directed Moses's attention to the fact that He will accompany him and help him in everything he had to do.

My friend, you will often find yourself faced with moments when your strength, ability and resources will seem insufficient before the mountain of problems standing before you. In those moments, fear might paralyze you, or you will receive strength from God Almighty. You will either allow yourself to be overtaken by doubt or you will advance confidently feeding from the unending fountain of His might. God is on your side, and He will turn on the light for you in the darkness. Move forward, relying on His resources and not on your own.

What I want from you on this day is to move forward with confidence as you rely on Me. If you feel pressed and low on energy, I will energize you. I will bless you and give you the strength to achieve with My help. Don't let the Evil One's voice repeat the same negative rhyme about what you don't have and what you cannot do. Rely on My power, and in what I have called you to do, rely on My unlimited resources. I will open a blessed door so you can see how I support you in what you do for Me.

But Moses said to God, "Who am I that I should go to Pharaoh and bring the Israelites out of Egypt?" And God said, "I will be with you..." – Exodus 3:11-12

So do not fear, for I am with you; do not be dismayed, for I am your God. I will strengthen you and help you; I will uphold you with my righteous right hand.
– Isaiah 41:10

68

THE CRUST OF SIN

For the word of God is alive and active. Sharper than any double-edged sword, it penetrates even to dividing soul and spirit, joints and marrow; it judges the thoughts and attitudes of the heart. – Hebrew 4:12

The rays of divine presence cannot enter a heart that is wrapped in the crust of sin. Sin is what will stop the manifestation of divine presence in man's life. Divine revelations, guidance for which a person prays, or His voice are stopped by sin. Isaiah said that sin is the separation wall between man and God, making prayer unable to reach Him.

The crust of sin that settles over man's heart must be broken with the sword of the Spirit, which is the Word of God. This sword penetrates and parts the soul and spirit, judges the heart's feelings and thoughts. When you stand before the Word and allow it to investigate your life, the heart's thoughts and intentions are revealed and analyzed in the light of the divine reflector. The Sprit's sword cracks the crust of sin; confessing sins knocks down the separation wall between man and God, and communication becomes free and without impediments. Let the path between you and God be beaten by the steps of holiness.

The things, attitudes, people and spirits that intercept the relationship between you and God must be cast aside. No one can run in the marathon of faith while their legs are tied with the ropes of sin. The more you reject the shiny temptations of sin trying to envelop you or when you cut the chains that bind you, the easier it will be to run. Your relationship with Him will be alive, personal, and the rays of His presence will light your life and your path. Without holiness, man cannot see God.

I do not want My relationship with you to be blocked by sin. I want to work in your life freely and for you to hear My voice. When the wall of sin is cast aside, that is when I work freely and joyfully, and you can hear My whisper. When you become a channel through which grace flows, My truth and My guidance will be revealed in and through your life into the lives of those around you. I love you, and I want to show you great wonders that you have not yet seen. Stay in the presence of My Word, and I will enlighten you.

But your iniquities have separated you from your God;
your sins have hidden his face from you,
so that he will not hear. – Isaiah 59:2

Therefore, since we are surrounded by such a huge crowd of witnesses to the life of faith, let us strip off every weight that slows us down, especially the sin that so easily trips us up. And let us run with endurance the race God has set before us. – Hebrew 12:1 (NLT)

69

Rely on Him

Some trust in chariots and some in horses, but we trust in the name of the Lord our God. They are brought to their knees and fall, but we rise up and stand firm. – Psalm 20:7-8

During your life, various people close to you will help you in certain situations. When this illusion falls apart before your eyes, you will learn that you must rely only on God. He will bring you to that point when your expectations will disintegrate so that you may learn that you cannot put your trust in man, but in God. The victory that comes from Him can come through a small number of people as well as through a large number. He can give you victory through unusual means in order to show you that solutions come when you rely on Him.

Gideon called the people to fight for their country, which was about to be occupied. Thirty-two thousand people came—a small army compared to the enemy's extensive army. God asked Gideon to send those who were afraid home. Before his eyes 22,000 people melted away and went home. In the moment Gideon saw those turned backs and the boot prints in the mud, his illusions disintegrated. For the Israelites to march to war was normal because they were protecting their families and their possessions. However, God wanted to lead Gideon to the point where he relied solely on Him. Gideon's resounding victory was accomplished with a comparatively infinitesimal number of warriors to show him that reliance on God brings victory.

The place where the Lord wants you is to the point of full reliance on Him. That is where you will often arrive when your dreams fall apart, and people disappoint you. That is the place where you will best see divine power manifest in your situation. Disappointments and life's impossibilities are the scene where He works best and where you can experience His power.

Sometimes you will feel small and without resources when you see those around you relying on relationships, money and impressive resources. Never forget the God who created the heavens and the earth is on your side. Some truly rely on their horses and their imposing chariots, but you rely on Me. You will see how they fall, but you will remain standing because you stand next to Me and rely on Me. Do not become sad and disheartened when people turn their backs on you; I am on your side, and that's what's most important.

Now announce to the army, "Anyone who trembles with fear may turn back and leave Mount Gilead."
So, twenty-two thousand men left, while ten thousand remained. – Judges 7:3

The LORD is my rock, my fortress and my deliverer; my God is my rock, in whom I take refuge, my shield and the horn of my salvation, my stronghold. – Psalm 18:2

70

CALLING BACK THROUGH BLESSINGS

He said, "Throw your net on the right side of the boat and you will find some." When they did, they were unable to haul the net in because of the large number of fish. Then the disciple whom Jesus loved said to Peter, "It is the Lord!" – John 21:6-7

Life's crises will sometimes shake you, causing you to abandon what you were doing for the Lord. You will be tempted to turn your life's switch to another direction. In that moment you feel like you are sinking in the deep waters of uncertainty, you will feel betrayed by God. The Almighty One who should have been on your side should have done something for you.

Peter went through such a moment when he shifted and steered his life back to his old profession. Jesus had died, leaving them alone, and what they had imagined had not been fulfilled. So, he went fishing with the other disciples, feeling how his dreams and expectations were disintegrating. After a night of toil without catching any fish, Jesus showed up on the shore and told them: *"Throw the net out to the right side of the ship."*

A large school of fish miraculously entered into the discouraged disciples' net. Right away, the disciple John looked at their night-long toil alongside the blessing that came so quickly and miraculously and understood that the One who had spoken to them on the shore was Jesus. John recognized God's fingerprints in the blessing they had received. The blessing He gave them was meant to turn them back to Him. The miraculous blessing was the indicator directing them back to the Giver, to God.

One of the methods that the Lord will use in your life will be to call you back to Him through blessings—even some miraculous ones. Like the Lord used this method in His wayward disciple, He will use this design in your life as well. When you feel like you have fallen into failure, He will call you back through blessings. Oftentimes, despite the failures you will experience, the Lord has a much bigger plan than the one you can currently understand. He knows how to draw us back from our failures and show us His plan that goes beyond our understanding and delusions.

Some expect that the Lord will apply a drastic method, perhaps even punishment; however, He is filled with love and compassion. Have you seen His call to you through the blessings and favors that He has granted you? The doors that miraculously opened for you that you didn't deserve or expect are the signs of His love for you. Look beyond the blessings you receive and see that they come from God. Read the prints of His love for you daily in your life.

I want to surprise you with the blessings that I will place in your path. I know where the schools of fish are, and I can direct them into your nets. What I want you to see is that the blessing comes directly from Me as a sign of My love. Do not love the gift more than you love the Giver—Me. If I act with kindness and love toward the people who have distanced themselves from Me, how should you behave toward them? My child, smile at a sorrowful soul today.

When he was at the table with them, he took bread, gave thanks, broke it and began to give it to them. Then their eyes were opened, and they recognized him, and he disappeared from their sight.
– Luke 24:30-31

He asked her, "Woman, why are you crying? Who is it you are looking for?" Thinking he was the gardener, she said, "Sir, if you have carried him away, tell me where you have put him, and I will get him." Jesus said to her, "Mary." She turned toward him and cried out in Aramaic, "Rabboni!" (which means "Teacher").
– John 20:15-16

71

AFTER THE VICTORIES

No temptation has overtaken you except what is common to mankind. And God is faithful; he will not let you be tempted beyond what you can bear. But when you are tempted, he will also provide a way out so that you can endure it. – 1 Corinthians 1:13

After the mountain of victory, the trap of temptations will always come. The victory that you fought so hard to earn will produce ecstasy on one hand, and on the other hand, inattention. The ecstasy of accomplishment produces a feeling of confidence within you, causing you to become inattentive to the traps that the Evil One sets for you. The Devil wants to steal the joy of your victory and capsize you in the murky waters of sin and disappointment. Therefore, be attentive; keep your guard up for after every mountain (the victory), there is also a valley. We often fall into the valley because we rest on the laurels of victory and because of the emotional effort we dedicated to attaining victory.

Noah worked with his family for many, many years while building the ark. He listened to the Lord's command, overcame the mockery of people in society and managed to get through the flood. He had experienced a great victory. He came out victorious from constructing the ark; however, at the turn of the corner, the cliff of temptation awaited him. Noah got drunk, removed all of his clothing and one of his sons saw him in this state of undress. After victory, temptation awaits the inattentive.

Always be attentive to the danger of spiritual relaxation—the moment when you open the door and allow the Evil One to enter and conquer the joy of victory. Always keep your guard up because your Enemy, the Devil, is lurking around. His strategy will often be the lion's roar that sounds threatening to you; at other times it will be the serpent's hiss that comes subtly to deceive you. Stay vigilant and be alert to resist the temptations that try to throw you from the mountain of victory into the abyss of failure. Protect the taste of victories past by being spiritually vigilant and living alongside the Lord.

Victory comes from Me. I am the One who blesses you, and I help you move forward. Always be vigilant and watch for the traps that the Evil One sets for you. If you stay in My presence, I will help you calibrate your thoughts and emotions that sometimes run ahead like unruly horses. When you stay in the light of My Word, I will encourage you to do what you have to do, to guard yourself and to get ahead in all aspects of life. I love you, and I will give you strength and vigilance. I want to enjoy You celebrating the next victory.

Be alert and of sober mind. Your enemy the devil prowls around like a roaring lion looking for someone to devour. – 1 Peter 5:8

Therefore put on the full armor of God, so that when the day of evil comes, you may be able to stand your ground, and after you have done everything, to stand.
– Ephesians 6:13

72

Do Not Try to Help God

"For my thoughts are not your thoughts, neither are your ways my ways," declares the LORD. "As the heavens are higher than the earth, so are my ways higher than your ways and my thoughts than your thoughts." – Isaiah 55:8-9

When God promises, that promise creates enthusiasm and will undoubtedly be fulfilled. However, if that promise does not materialize in the time that you imagine, you will sometimes become worried, impatient, and you will begin to seek solutions to help the divine plan. God does not need help to fulfill His promises. When you try to help Him to fulfill His promises, you often ruin the plan and run into problems. Wait for the time established by Him.

Abraham received the promise that a great nation would descend from him. His was a beautiful promise; however, his wife Sarah had reached an advanced age and could not bear children. Instead of waiting for God to do the impossible and fulfill what He had promised, Sarah came up with the idea for her to have a child by using her servant girl as a surrogate. She wanted to help God fulfill His promise, but her plan created more pain than solutions.

Perhaps you too expect certain things promised by Him to take place in your life. You will often notice that impatience and temptation to find solutions to help God will circle your mind like vultures. Resist the temptation to get ahead of the time established by Him. Certainly, God has a part to perform and man has his part to do, but do not try to do God's part, leaving your part undone.

Finding human solutions for the fulfillment of divine promises will ultimately bring regrets. When you try to fulfill His part, you will usually ruin aspects of the divine plan that you will later regret. God likes to work in life's impossible situations to make it obvious that His hand was at play. Wait for the time, methods, and solutions decided by Him.

When you get the idea to help Me to fulfill my plan, may I remind you that thought does not come from Me. Wait with patience. I want to order my plan. Do not rush. I know the right time for My promises to be fulfilled in your life. When you are in the time of waiting, you are, in fact, in My school where I am preparing you to be useful and ready for what I will do in your life. I am more interested in what you will become than in the gift you will receive.

The LORD Almighty has sworn, "Surely, as I have planned, so it will be, and as I have purposed, so it will happen. – Isaiah 14:24

"I will make you into a great nation, and I will bless you; I will make your name great, and you will be a blessing. – Genesis 12:2

73

BE ALERT TO MY PATHS

God works in different ways, but it is the same God who does the work in all of us. – 1 Corinthians 12:6 (NLT)

Some days will seem routine to you—like a beaten path that you have walked along many times. Other days will seem like blazing a trail through the forest—taking a new road that you've never set foot on before. Throughout life's zigzags, new and unexpected happenings will demand your attention and often cause confusion. At those times be alert to God's plan, which often develops in ways different than you would expect. Many people feel good staying in their familiar daily routine; however, what the Lord wants is for you to be open to the new and understand the movement of His hand in your life. Certainly, you will only understand the full extent of certain matters later on. However, like a surfer catching a wave, be attentive to the work that God wants to perform within a certain context. The surfer awaits, tensely attentive, to catch the wave that rises, and then he lets himself be taken where the wave leads him. Be like the surfer, letting God take you where He will.

General Naaman needed healing. When the prophet Elijah sent him a message to go to Jordan and bathe there seven times, the general refused, and still plagued by the leprosy, he almost returned home. He was repelled by the fact that the River Jordan was dirty compared to those pristine waters in his own country. Neither did he appreciate the fact that Elijah had not respected his lofty position according to social etiquette. The general almost rejected his moment of healing because he was not alert to the new method that God had chosen to use for him. His servants convinced him to do anything to "catch the wave"—that special moment. Naaman finally listened, and thus, he was healed of leprosy.

Many people remained trapped in a method they expected or imposed upon God to use for their lives. Many lost certain works or divine actions because they were not alert to what He does. Be satisfied to wait so that the Lord may work using both old and new methods. He works sometimes in one way, sometimes in another, but people generally do not realize the way He is working.

The more you spend time in fellowship with the Lord, the more alert and attentive you will be in understanding when you see His hand at work. You will begin to develop a particular sensitivity to understanding and more easily accept His doing something that goes beyond what you were used to.

The same is true with solving some issues in your life. You often expect your problem to be solved in the way that you think; however, the solution often comes in an unexpected way or by unexpected means. What the Lord expects from you is a spiritual alertness toward the way He chooses to unfold His plan.

I work in different ways. I like to go beyond labels or methods that seem normal and appropriate to you. I want you to develop an alertness toward My actions and recognize when I intercede in a different way. During this time, stay alert and attentive because I want to speak to you, and I want to solve certain situations in your life in a different way than you think.

Truly, O God of Israel, our Savior, you work in mysterious ways. – Isaiah 45:15 (NLT)

For God does speak—now one way, now another-- though no one perceives it. – Job 33:14

*Trust in the L*ORD *with all your heart and lean not on your own understanding; in all your ways submit to him, and he will make your paths straight.*
– Proverbs 3:5-6

74

YOUR LIFE'S TEMPLE

Do you not know that you are God's temple and that God's Spirit dwells in you? – 1 Corinthians 3:16 (ESV)

The only temple where God resides here on earth is in a believer's life. Your life is His temple where He likes to live to guide you and whisper to you of His great love. The way He walked through the garden of Eden and spoke to Adam and Eve in the quiet of the morning is how He wants to walk in the garden of your heart and speak to you.

When Jesus entered the temple in Jerusalem, He expected to hear the voice of the Father there. Instead, He found a great deal of chatter and noise. He could hear the sounds of animals, the sound of money and the voices of merchants buying and selling. The temple where the Lord's voice should have been housed had been transformed into a cave of thieves.

Your body is the Holy Spirit's temple. Many voices compete to be heard and to dominate the temple of your life. Many of these voices seem favorable, but what the Lord wants is for you to have moments of silence when you hear only His voice. When you share solitude and quiet with Him, your ear starts to set to the frequency of heaven. In that quiet, you will begin to hear the song of heaven, and you will be flooded by His divine presence. His light will reach into all the corners of your heart.

He wants to speak to you in the sanctuary of your spirit. In the time that you spend with Him, silence the voices that urgently call you to complete your tasks. The time spent in His presence is not wasted as others will try to make you believe; rather, this time is valuable for you to revitalize and to become familiar with the song of heaven. That song will strengthen you, give you direction, clarity, and help you become more efficient in what you have to do.

The walk you take with Me in the temple of your life is the most important part of your day. My voice to guide you daily can be heard there, and I want to speak to you, advise you and bless you. Make room for quiet in your life. Train your ear to hear Me, and you will see how My voice will become clearer and clearer. I use this significant method to speak to you about My plans that I want to declare to you.

Who, then, are those who fear the LORD? He will instruct them in the ways they should choose.
– Psalm 25:12

Do you not know that your bodies are temples of the Holy Spirit, who is in you, whom you have received from God? You are not your own; you were bought at a price. Therefore, honor God with your bodies.
– 1 Corinthians 6:19-20

75

REBUILD THE ALTAR
OF PRAISE

Then Elijah called to the people, "Come over here!" They all crowded around him as he repaired the altar of the LORD that had been torn down. He took twelve stones, one to represent each of the tribes of Israel. – 1 Kings 18:30-31 (NLT)

In the lives of many believers, the altar of prayer lies in ruins. Many hearts dedicate their time and energy to the idols of materialism and pleasures, and the altar of prayer is abandoned. The idols of this world have caused many to run in a hamster wheel that leads nowhere from eternity's point of view. The soul remains starving like an arid land, thirsty for God.

God is seeking people to fix the altar of prayer and keep the flame of prayer burning. The time you will spend before the altar of prayer will bring you closer to Him and, at the same time, bring spiritual healing for you, and those around you will be fueled by this prayer.

Elijah saw the nation become idolatrous and the altar of praise in ruins. He took the step of courage in that idolatrous society and called the people to see him bringing an offering. Before their eyes, he placed 12 stones (to depict the unity of the 12 tribes of Israel) to reconstruct the altar. He called people to bring water and pour it over the offering he placed on the altar during the period of drought, picturing sacrifice.

You will also need these three elements of courage, sacrifice, and unity to rebuild the altar of praise. Courage comes from the guidance you receive when you walk alongside Him and know His presence. Each step you take alongside the LORD will build greater trust within you, as well as the confidence to advance in connection with Him.

Sacrifice comes from the offerings it costs. When you sacrifice yourself for the Lord, you are placing a pleasant offering on the altar of praise. When you do something for Him, you are bringing a sacrifice to honor Him.

Unity, which is needed to rebuild, is the act of humbleness that makes you renounce arrogance to keep the living stones that build the altar together.

Courage, sacrifice, and unity will rebuild the altar of praise in your life and your family. The time that you will put aside for the Lord will be a special time that will attract His presence and His peace.

When you start to build an altar for Me, do not forget your need for courage to stand against the currents and idolatry around you. All My people who went against the current were marked by courage. I want to remind you that I did not remain indebted to anyone, and the sacrifice that you make for Me shall be repaid. Stand in unity alongside Me. Seek people who understand these eternal values as well. I will open your eyes so that you may see other people who work on the altar of praise, and I will connect you with them.

Make every effort to keep the unity of the Spirit through the bond of peace. – Ephesians 4:3

Therefore, I urge you, brothers and sisters, in view of God's mercy, to offer your bodies as a living sacrifice, holy and pleasing to God—this is your true and proper worship. – Romans 12:1

76

LATER ON, YOU WILL UNDERSTAND

You intended to harm me, but God intended it for good to accomplish what is now being done, the saving of many lives. – Genesis 50:20

You will only understand certain events that happened in your life at a later time. With the passing of time, you will look at what has happened in retrospect and start to see how each piece of the puzzle will fall into place. During the storm or the thick of the fog, understanding the direction in which the divine hand moves it is difficult. However, once the storm has calmed or the fog has settled, and you replay the movie of the events, you will see God's purpose for your favor.

Joseph didn't understand why his brothers had sold him as a slave. He didn't understand why he had to be unjustly accused and imprisoned. For 13 years, all things were seemingly against him. However, after those years, God "flipped the switch," and Joseph was promoted from being a prisoner to be the vice-pharaoh of Egypt. In saving his family from death by starvation, he understood that the Almighty had sent him there with a purpose.

Perhaps you too are at a period when events and people are seemingly against you. Do not forget that God is on your side, for at the right time, He will turn things to your favor. Just like Joseph, you will later understand that God had a plan prepared even in that difficult period of your life. He allows you to go through certain events with a specific purpose that you will later understand. Looking back, you will ascertain His divine plan. Patience is an active ingredient in the composition of faith.

Perhaps you are currently in the midst of certain events that you do not understand, and what is happening makes absolutely no sense. I would like to remind you that I am on your side. Soon, you will be able to look back and understand that My hand was at work in your favor and in accordance with My plan. Believe in Me because I have good plans for you and trust Me as you walk in life's foggy moments while listening to My voice. Stay with faith and satisfaction even in life's difficult moments.

But now, this is what the LORD says—he who created you, Jacob, he who formed you, Israel: "Do not fear, for I have redeemed you; I have summoned you by name; you are mine. When you pass through the waters, I will be with you; and when you pass through the rivers, they will not sweep over you. When you walk through the fire, you will not be burned; the flames will not set you ablaze. – Isaiah 43:1-2

77

DISADVANTAGES ARE MY TOOLS

But he said to me, "My grace is sufficient for you, for my power is made perfect in weakness." Therefore, I will boast all the more gladly about my weaknesses, so that Christ's power may rest on me. – 2 Corinthians 12:9

Life's disadvantages are the scene where God works with power.

For many people, these unexpected disadvantages produce suffering and sorrow; however, He uses them in His divine plan to accomplish some grand plans. Each lack or pain that you feel has a role in God's divine plan.

Even if the Evil One has attacked you and produced suffering, do not forget that the Lord can change suffering and disadvantage to reveal His power.

He has created or allowed all things for a purpose. He has created your strong points, your abilities and skills with a purpose in mind, but He has also left some deficiencies in your life. Do not let life's drawbacks sadden you. You must understand and accept that He has given you deficiencies for a determined purpose. You must be alert to the methods through which He works and what He wants to accomplish through any disadvantage remaining in your life.

The citadel of Samaria had been attacked. No one was going in or out of the fortification. Famine loomed for months throughout the citadel, and the situation was catastrophic.

Four lepers lived outside the citadel because of their physical condition. Within their small leper colony, even greater famine had taken place. These four decided to venture into the enemy encampment to obtain something to eat. They did not know God had frightened away the enemy who had left behind all their provisions. The lepers realized that their discovery marked a day of victory, and they should also go to their compatriots at the citadel of Samaria to share the good news. The four lepers, even at a disadvantage in their condition, had saved the citadel of Samaria. They had likely saved their own wives and children from starvation. The disease that had brought them much sorrow and suffering was used by God as a divine instrument; they became the announcers of salvation.

Perhaps you too do not understand why you have endured certain disadvantages in life that bother you greatly. Do not forget that God uses people with great disadvantages to accomplish great works so that all of the glory and grace may go to Him.

If you have unfortunate disadvantages, wait and see. Be attentive so that you may understand how He will use those things for His grace and glory. Do not allow life's disadvantages to throw you in the corner of spiritual sorrow; rather, seek to see how you will be an instrument within His divine plan. God uses weak things in the world to put the powerful ones to shame.

I want you to understand that My designing hands have purposely allowed certain deficiencies, questions, and situations in your life that you won't always under-

stand but have a purpose within My plan. Parts that appear negative have a role in My plan to uplift other people, to bring life, hope, and salvation. Do not allow the negative aspects to bring you sorrow; rather, put them in My service so that they may bear fruit.

That is why, for Christ's sake, I delight in weaknesses, in insults, in hardships, in persecutions, in difficulties. For when I am weak, then I am strong.
– 2 Corinthians 12:10

The men who had leprosy reached the edge of the camp, entered one of the tents and ate and drank. Then they took silver, gold and clothes, and went off and hid them. They returned and entered another tent and took some things from it and hid them also. Then they said to each other, "What we're doing is not right. This is a day of good news and we are keeping it to ourselves. If we wait until daylight, punishment will overtake us. Let's go at once and report this to the royal palace."
– 2 Kings 7:8-9

78

Plow a New Field

Sow your seed in the morning, and at evening let your hands not be idle, for you do not know which will succeed, whether this or that, or whether both will do equally well. – Ecclesiastes 11:6

In life, people tend to do only what they are certain will bring them profit. They tend to invest their time and energy in only the seed that brings them fruit. On one hand, this attention and investment will be beneficial; on the other hand, the singlemindedness can limit their life.

Solomon, the wisest man who lived, introduced the idea that the seed should be planted in multiple directions or fields because no one knows for sure what will bear fruit. Perhaps you will get fruit from only one part or perhaps you will have fruit from multiple sides. Having the fruit come from multiple places would be advantageous.

Resolve today to work with a diligent hand and not limit yourself to only one filed. Pray before the Lord for light and guidance to understand where to invest your energy and time. Pray for diligence and strength to plan in different fields. God encourages you to sow the seeds of a new investment.

Your work is praise before Me. I want to bless you in

what you do, and I want you to invest in new perspectives I prepare. Why limit yourself to little, when I have prepared a lot for you? Whether you plant the seed in My field or in the field of your daily work, I will bless it so that it may bear fruit. Invest in multiple directions and plant at the right time, I will make it bear fruit.

Sow righteousness for yourselves, reap the fruit of unfailing love, and break up your unplowed ground; for it is time to seek the LORD, until he comes and showers his righteousness on you. – Hosea 10:12

I planted the seed, Apollos watered it, but God has been making it grow. – 1 Corinthians 3:6

An unplowed field produces food for the poor, but injustice sweeps it away.
– Proverbs 13:23

79

I Am With You

Yet I am always with you; you hold me by my right hand.
– Psalm 73:23

In your loneliness, you can feel My presence in an outstanding way.

Even if there are hundreds and thousands of people who pass by you and are around you, you might often feel alone. Feeling an overwhelming loneliness in the presence of people is painful. May I remind you that your Best Friend—Jesus—is beside you at all times. His presence can be felt in an outstanding way when you sit and talk to Him. Many people run away from loneliness, embracing packed schedules, living a noisy life filled with fatigue. They surround themselves with many friends to allay loneliness, but that feeling does not go away through avoidance or evasion.

Feelings of loneliness will only be defeated through dialogue with the Lord. If loneliness overwhelms you, speak to the Lord more. With each conversation you have with Him, His presence will be felt more and more; thus, the feelings of loneliness will disappear. The more you become aware that He is beside you and wants to speak to you in the same way that you converse with a friend, the more the loneliness will dissipate, and the joy of that relationship will appear. Make it a habit to walk with God through the garden of your life, and loneliness will disappear.

I am close to you; I love you with an eternal love. Talk to Me more, and little by little, you will notice Me at every step and feel My closeness. You will begin to feel My presence more in every circumstance. What I want from you with each day is to speak to Me like you speak to a friend and become aware of My presence with you.

A father to the fatherless, a defender of widows, is God in his holy dwelling. God sets the lonely in families, he leads out the prisoners with singing; but the rebellious live in a sun-scorched land. – Psalm 68:5-6

…and teaching them to obey everything I have commanded you. And surely I am with you always, to the very end of the age. – Matthew 28:20

Though my father and mother forsake me, the LORD *will receive me.* – Psalm 27:10

80

PERFECT PEACE

You will keep in perfect peace those whose minds are steadfast, because they trust in you. – Isaiah 26:3

The thoughts on which you ruminate will influence your emotions. Peace or worry, spiritual calm or pressing stress are the product of what your mind contemplates. Thoughts knock on your mind's door every moment, wanting to enter and set up a nest. Do not let thoughts of worry embed your mind's chamber. Think of peace and spiritual calm. Meditate on His Words and tell of His wonders. Do not give ground to the pressing thoughts and worries that want to trap you in their net.

Isaiah said that if you trust in the Lord and concentrate your thoughts on Him, then His peace will invade your soul. When you start your day by setting your gaze upon the Lord who prepares the path before your steps, you will start the day with peace and joy. When you set your thoughts upon the One who is on His eternal royal throne, you start to gain confidence and advance with a lot of courage.

Set your soul's gaze toward Me, looking at Me through faith. See how I fight for you within the unseen world. Notice how I open doors for you and favor you before other people. When you look into My eyes, peace begins to envelop you, and joy begins to flow like a holy, scented oil over your head. I am beside you and want you to step forward on this day, knowing that you are My favored son or daughter.

Therefore, holy brothers and sisters, who share in the heavenly calling, fix your thoughts on Jesus, whom we acknowledge as our apostle and high priest.
– Hebrew 3:1

Set your minds on things above, not on earthly things.
– Colossians 3:2

81

OVERCOME OBSTACLES

Since they could not get him to Jesus because of the crowd, they made an opening in the roof above Jesus by digging through it and then lowered the mat the man was lying on. – Mark 2:4

Along the road of your life, obstacles will sometimes arise that will prevent you from reaching the goal you've set for yourself. These difficulties may cause you to capitulate, or they can make you more determined and energize you to advance as you experience divine assistance.

Giving up is not an option when you know that His specific will is for you to complete a specific ministry or reach a certain objective. God's wish for you is not to give up when faced with obstacles that you encounter because He is your support and your help. He supports you in reaching your aim, either by avoiding certain situations or by giving you strength to withstand those difficult situations. In the life of faith, you must experience the victory resulting from divine intervention.

Four people took their sick, bedridden friend to Jesus. Because of the crowd gathered in the house listening to the Redeemer, their access was blocked. I find it amazing that the friends did not give up when faced with this obstacle. On the contrary, they lifted the bed up to the top of the house and broke through the roof to lower the sick man's bed in front of Jesus. Their determination, persistence and courage against the barriers helped the ailing man receive healing. Jesus praises the faith of the four people who persisted despite the obstacles they encountered.

If you find yourself faced with certain obstacles or problems, remember that the Lord is on your side. He is your help in need. He will give you strength to persevere, and He will open your supernatural eyes to find the solution you need. When the day's stubborn problems whisper "Yield" or "Give up" to you, proclaim the Lord's might and presence which is beside you and helps you win. Proclaim: *"I can do everything through Christ who strengthens me."*

Instead of letting life's obstacles get you down, transform them into teaching incidents that can grow your faith, instruct you, and motivate you to seek supernatural solutions. Do not yield in the face of obstacles; the Lord is on your side. He is your support in what you need to do on this day.

If you draw the sap of your courage from My might and My presence, you will win. One day, you will plant the flag of victory that I will give you on the land of the problems that you are facing. On that flag it will say, "The Lord is my strength and my courage."

Take steps alongside of Me. Do not let yourself be overwhelmed by the problem nagging you. Speak to Me constantly, stay in touch with Me, and I will advise you as to how you must move forward. Do not try to carry the mountain of problems on your own back because you will be spiritually weakened. Constantly hand it over to

Me. Submitting the problem to Me will keep your mind and soul healthy in the midst of adversities. I am with you, and I will not abandon you. You will soon look back at the difficult time you experienced with My help, and you will thank Me. I have prepared a victory flag for you that I want you to wave in My name.

I lift up my eyes to the mountains—where does my help come from? My help comes from the LORD, the Maker of heaven and earth. He will not let your foot slip—he who watches over you will not slumber. – Psalm 121:1-3

I have told you these things, so that in me you may have peace. In this world you will have trouble. But take heart! I have overcome the world. – John 16:33

82

INVEST IN A LETTER

You show that you are a letter from Christ, the result of our ministry, written not with ink but with the Spirit of the living God, not on tablets of stone but on tablets of human hearts. – 2 Corinthians 3:3

You are the letter that the LORD wrote with His love that is read by those around you. Your life is part of the library of the world and, your book contains the victories, challenges, and facts of faith that you have experienced. Those who read the lines in your life's letter must see your faith and feel encouraged.

On the other hand, you are also a writer who prints God's Words on the hearts of those around you. Writing "faith" in the hearts of those near you is like making an investment in the letter of hope that you send into the world, which will later lift up those who read it. You do not work on these letters with ink, but with God's Holy Spirit.

The apostle Paul, in his time, worked on the letter that was directed to the people of Corinth. He was proud of them because he had put the words of Truth in their hearts.

The investment that you make when you place the words of Truth in the hearts of those around you is an investment in a living epistle of flesh and blood, which goes into the world to spread the message of hope. God likes these types of investments, and He repays them. Be the chisel for the Holy Ghost to use in carving faith and hope in the hearts of those around you. I leave you with this question: in what letter are you investing? In which hearts have you placed the words of the Scripture? What letter of hope are you preparing to send into this world where so many are disoriented and unloved?

My friend, put the words of eternal life into a person's heart this week. Pray for someone in whom you can write the words of eternal life.

The words of faith that you write into people's hearts are the investment that you will encounter in eternity. My Spirit will support you when everything you have done seems to be of no use and shows no results. Do not be discouraged; continue laying My words in the hearts and minds of those around you. Later on, you will see its fruit. When you fulfill My will, I bless and repay you. In this crowded world chasing after material possessions and pleasures, do not feel like the investment you make in My work is a waste of time. Put My Words in as many hearts as possible so that the message of faith might spread and reach those who have no hope. This is a way of growing the kingdom of Light.

You yourselves are our letter, written on our hearts, known and read by everyone. – 2 Corinthians 3:2

I will give them an undivided heart and put a new spirit in them; I will remove from them their heart of stone and give them a heart of flesh. Then they will follow my decrees and be careful to keep my laws. They will be my people, and I will be their God.
– Ezekiel 11:10-20

83

The Oil of Joy

As dead flies give perfume a bad smell, so a little folly outweighs wisdom and honor. – Ecclesiastes 10:1

Joy must be an active part of your life. God constantly pours the oil of joy and joviality in order to give you enthusiasm and energize your life. This oil must be kept clean to be used to its fullest effect.

If you leave a few dead flies in a bottle of scented oil, they will spoil and ruin the scent. Likewise, if you allow "flies" access to the oil of joy that the Lord pours into your life, your joy will be ruined. Place the oil of your life before the divine reflector—His Word—to show you the harmful "insects" of bitterness, sorrows, displeasures, worry, unforgiveness, negative thoughts. Ask God to cleanse the oil.

If a fresh anointing of oil comes over you, these same "insects" will spoil the oil. Scan your life and remove all of the aspects that can taint your joy. Guard your life from harmful "insects" the Evil One wants to use to contaminate your life.

On today's road of life, emanate the perfume of joy and divine presence wherever you go. Take with you the freshness of His divine presence, allowing the oil of joy to flow from your life. Its lovely scented perfume will permeate the lives of others as well.

In My presence, you will find satisfaction, and your joy will grow and flow from your life like a river. Spend time inhaling the clean air of heaven, and your life will be energized through My presence. Your decisions will be marked by My advice, and your hands will be blessed in everything they undertake. Guard the oil of your joy from the useless particles that can contaminate it. Guard your heart's garden from the negative seeds that the Evil One wants to plant through various people. Everything that goes into your life must first go through My presence. Invite Me to take a walk through the garden of your heart. Let's sit down, talk and spend that wonderful time together that can bring you closer to My love—to heaven.

You make known to me the path of life; you will fill me with joy in your presence, with eternal pleasures at your right hand. – Psalm 16:11

You have loved righteousness and hated wickedness; therefore God, your God, has set you above your companions by anointing you with the oil of joy.
– Hebrews 1:9

May the God of hope fill you with all joy and peace as you trust in him, so that you may overflow with hope by the power of the Holy Spirit. – Romans 15:13

84

TAKING CARE

On coming to the house, they saw the child with his mother Mary, and they bowed down and worshiped him. Then they opened their treasures and presented him with gifts of gold, frankincense and myrrh. – Matthew 2:11

Before life's events take place, God already knows them ahead of time. He knows what will be on your life's calendar, He knows what you need, and He prepares the necessary resources. He sees the attacks that the Evil One designs, and He prepares an escape door to give you access to the castle of divine protection. His protection for you is real and, at a given moment, you will experience it in an untold way. Stay constantly connected to divine guidance. When you stay in contact with the Lord, He advises you and shows you the path to walk on.

The Magi followed the path of the guiding start that led them to the newborn King. They bowed to Jesus and gave Him gifts of gold, symbolizing His royalty, gifts of myrrh symbolizing the fact that He would be the sacrifice for the sins of mankind, and frankincense symbolizing the fact that He was a priest.

That extremely valuable gift of gold, brought from a great distance, was God's solution for a difficult situation that Joseph, Mary and the infant Jesus would experience. God knew of Herod's insane envy, who upon hearing that a new king was born, sent his soldiers with ready swords to find Jesus.

In a dream at night, God spoke to Joseph, the young father, telling him that he should take Mary and Jesus and flee to Egypt. Newly married, Joseph had just returned from a short trip to his native village to complete the census. Now this? How would he survive in the foreign country of Egypt? Unknown to Joseph, God had already prepared by sending the Magi from thousands of miles away to bring them gold, a necessary resource to save the plan for salvation, to save them from Herod's bloody sword, and to hide them under His wing.

In your life before you go through various challenges, He will have already prepared the necessary resources and the solutions to help you. He sees beyond what you see and has prepared your escape door to hide you in the castle of divine protection. God cares about you and does not want you to fall into the net or into the traps of the Evil One. Stay in touch with Him, and He will guide you to the next step. This will be a day when you will walk protected and guarded by the protective shield of the LORD. Thank Him for taking care of you.

I have the best plans for you. These will come to fruition when you are alert to My whisper. Even if the Evil One makes plans against you, I will protect you, guard you, and put the Enemy to shame. I love you, and I want you to live in victory and to walk with your head held high because I am on your side. Remember on this day that I, the God of the universe, love you, support you, and guide you. I will send you the necessary resources that you will need for the challenges ahead. Pray to understand the roles of the resources that I have given you as part of My plan. Trust in Me, and you will experience great things.

But I will sing of your strength, in the morning I will sing of your love; for you are my fortress, my refuge in times of trouble. – Psalm 59:16

My God is my rock, in whom I take refuge, my shield and the horn of my salvation. He is my stronghold, my refuge and my savior—from violent people you save me. – 2 Samuel 22:3

85

MIRACLES AND DILIGENCE

The LORD your God has blessed you in all the work of your hands. He has watched over your journey through this vast wilderness. These forty years the LORD your God has been with you, and you have not lacked anything. – Deuteronomy 2:7

Divine blessing will be revealed in your life in various ways. How the LORD will do the revealing is His decision, but you must believe and wait in every season for when He chooses to pour the rain of heavenly and earthly blessings over your life.

The Hebrew people, who wandered through the desert for forty years, saw many miracles—the manna that fed them daily, the shoe bindings that did not wear out for 40 years, and the enemy strongholds that fell miraculously before them. Miracles were the method God used in the desert that His people crossed.

When the children of Israel reached the Promised Land, God took care of them using the natural laws, their diligence and obedience. The supernatural manna ended; however, He blessed their hard work and caused the earth to give them bountiful fruit.

When you go through episodes of desert in life, remember

that He has already prepared supernatural solutions to help you get through the difficult times. The Lord is always beside you and will make springs of water gush in deserted places. He will turn hard rock into springs of water because He is the God of miracles.

When you will reach the *Promised Land*, when you receive blessed positions in your place of employment or the Lord places you in positions of potential, do not forget to be diligent. He will make your work bear rich fruit and, through that fruit, He will show you the sign of divine blessings. The Lord will make the land that you plow give plentiful fruit.

Look deeply and notice His prints in the blessings that you have received.

Stand beside Me in any of life's seasons. When the land of your life is going through a drought, do not forget that I can create water springs even in deserted places. Those will be unique moments when you will experience My miracles in a phenomenal way. Do not allow the unknowns of today or tomorrow cause you sorrow; I already know it. Everything is exposed and uncovered before Me. Trust in Me and be confident that I know what you need. As you enter your wilderness, know that I have prepared all of the necessary resources for you. I have arranged for people to help you during life's difficult times. In My presence, you will receive the strength to move forward through life's unknowns. I walk alongside you.

For forty years you sustained them in the wilderness; they lacked nothing, their clothes did not wear out nor did their feet become swollen. – Nehemiah 9:21

The LORD will indeed give what is good, and our land will yield its harvest. – Psalm 85:12

For the LORD God is a sun and shield; the LORD bestows favor and honor; no good thing does he withhold from those whose walk is blameless. – Psalm 84:11

86

PARALYZED BY THE PAST

Brothers and sisters, I do not consider myself yet to have taken hold of it. But one thing I do: Forgetting what is behind and straining toward what is ahead, I press on toward the goal to win the prize for which God has called me heavenward in Christ Jesus. – Philippians 3:13-14

For many, the past is a thief of joy and enthusiasm.

If you look into your past, in all likelihood, you will see some situations that you should not have done or handled differently. Perhaps you remember words that you should not have spoken and decisions that you should not have made as you had. For many, the past is soaked in the waters of regret, and this water has a dreadful smell.

Many consume their energy, trying to reach an understanding and coming to terms with their past, without success. They forget that God has forgiveness and grace for the past, present and future and that they were forgiven in Jesus Christ's sacrifice.

If you can change something from your past, change it. If you cannot, do as the apostle Paul, who did not allow himself to be harassed by the mistakes of the past, but received forgiveness for his past and launched himself toward the prize that awaited him.

When the Evil One tries to accuse you of past mistakes, remind him of his future and proclaim the forgiveness that you have received. The Lord has grace for your present, past and future.

The Lord's plans for your life are great and wonderful. Look ahead to the future with confidence and allow yourself to feel enthusiasm for what He will do for you. Do not allow yourself to be stuck in the prison of the past where the Evil One wants to lock you up. Proclaim that your future alongside the LORD is filled with light and with wonderful plans that I cannot wait to experience.

The plans that I have for you can often be rendered useless because the sorrows of the past envelop you. I have forgiven you, and I do not want to remember what has happened. Look ahead and advance confidently. I love you, and I walk alongside you. I want you to discover My works and My blessings for you in the present, as well as in the future that lies ahead of you. Use your energy to work the fields of the Gospel; do not waste it trying to change what can no longer be changed or on the Evil One's accusations. When you speak to Me today, be freed from the past. I forgive you, and I have good plans for you. Cut the negative chains of the past and live freely.

Jesus replied, "No one who puts a hand to the plow and looks back is fit for service in the kingdom of God."
– Luke 9:62

For I know the plans I have for you," declares the LORD,
"plans to prosper you and not to harm you,
plans to give you hope and a future.
– Jeremiah 29:11

87

SPEAK TO YOUR SOUL

Why, my soul, are you downcast? Why so disturbed within me? Put your hope in God, for I will yet praise him, my Savior and my God. – Psalm 42:5

Have you ever descended into a state of sorrow and your soul felt dejected? I find that many people run through life without looking at the condition of their souls. Some continue along life's journey, ignoring their inner sorrows and limping along for an indeterminate amount of time. On the other hand, some people are far more attentive and take care of their inner state.

David was feeling down and stopped his life's race to speak to his soul: *"Why, my soul, are you downcast? Why so disturbed within me?"* The dialogue he began was intended to resolve some upsetting issues and also to correct the skewed perspectives through which he had begun to look at life.

When the check engine light illuminates the dashboard of your life, you must stop to ascertain the source of the issue. What is the cause of your stress and your pain? God's intention is for you to live an abundant spiritual life. Do not ignore the signals of the soul that tell you something is not quite right. Do not drive your life's car until you cause major damage or even quit running. Do not allow the tyrant of time or the standards imposed by others to have as many material possessions as possible force you into a race to accumulate. Only then will you realize that your starving soul is longing for the crumbs of divine presence.

Time spent in the presence of the Lord fills up your soul like rich and meaty food. Stop and rest in His presence. Trusting in Him in the midst of life's trails is the proof of rest in His presence. The solution for your soul is reliance on the Lord.

Do not let the thought that "things will always be this way" build a nest within you and develop. Remember that joy will come again, and you will praise Him. The Lord will open the floodgates of heaven and the abundance of joy will pour over you. Speak to your soul about His promises and encourage yourself that outstandingly good times will come in your life.

Some days will seem difficult and tiring. I want to remind you that I am on your side and, during those days, I want to energize you. I wish for joy, peace and hope to radiate in your life. Speak to yourself and encourage yourself with My promises. Do not let yourself be pressed down by fatigue. Treat your state of fatigue with rest by standing in My presence and eating the rich foods that I have prepared for you. I love you, and I want to revitalize you. Smile and lift up a sorrowful soul this week.

My soul will be satisfied as with fat and rich food, and my mouth will praise you with joyful lips, when I remember you upon my bed, and meditate on you in the watches of the night. - Psalm 63:5-6 (ESV)

Come to me, all you who are weary and burdened, and
I will give you rest. – Matthew 11:28

The Lord is close to the brokenhearted and saves those
who are crushed in spirit. – Psalm 34:18

88

THE SHOUT OF FAITH

When you hear them sound a long blast on the trumpets, have the whole army give a loud shout; then the wall of the city will collapse and the army will go up, everyone straight in. – Joshua 6:5

God gave Joshua a seemingly impossible mission: conquer the city of Jericho. The imposing walls, the lack of weapons, and their lack of experience made Jericho seem an insurmountable obstacle. Like the children of Israel, every believer will face an immovable Jericho or some obstacle that appears impossible to surpass at some point.

Joshua received a divine revelation telling him to surround the great city and, upon the shout of faith, the impossible walls would crumble and fall. From a human point of view, taking the city was a suicidal military strategy; however, from a divine point of view, they knew the solution for victory. Theirs was a divine solution to a human problem. That shout had to be the shout of faith. After seven days, upon their shout, the imposing walls cracked and fell before their eyes like a house of cards.

For you to see a solution in others' lives will be easier than for you to notice in your own life how problems create sorrow, cause you to worry and see all the drama of problems. However, the Lord wants you to speak of victory, practice the shout of faith—either out loud or within your spirit—and look through your spiritual eyes to see how the walls of the Jericho in your life come crashing down. Imagine through faith how the walls of the problem that is upsetting you will begin to crack and fall. Watch through the eyes of faith as you wave the flag of victory over the problem that presses on you. Jesus told the disciples, "If you would have faith, you would tell the mulberry tree to jump into the sea and it would jump."

Begin to practice the shout of victory and speak to the problems in your life through faith to make them come crashing down.

With the passing of time, you will see that you often turn to relationships or resources to solve the problem, but you will notice that everything you do will barely make a dent in a brick. However, the shout of faith, combined with the solution that God will reveal to you will bring you a great victory, and the problems will fall to the ground.

Your faith will not depend on human abilities, but on the Lord's power.

I am beside you, and I am accompanying you. Look through the eyes of faith at My shadow on your right hand. Do not let yourself be intimidated by the problems that come toward you but learn to face them together with Me. Develop reliance on My power in your life. Any victory that you have had alongside Me will develop your faith, and you will trust Me more and more. When the Jericho of impossibility will appear before you, practice the shout of faith. Stay connected to My resources and solutions, which are different for any situation. Then you will see the walls come crashing down.

*I keep my eyes always on the L*ORD*. With him at my right hand, I will not be shaken. – Psalm 16:8*

About midnight Paul and Silas were praying and singing hymns to God, and the other prisoners were listening to them. Suddenly there was such a violent earthquake that the foundations of the prison were shaken. At once all the prison doors flew open, and everyone's chains came loose. – Acts 16:25-26

89

AMBASSADORS

We are therefore Christ's ambassadors, as though God were making his appeal through us. We implore you on Christ's behalf: Be reconciled to God. – 2 Corinthians 5:20

You are in the privileged position of representing God on this earth. The ambassador is an extension of the King's hand in action. The ambassador is the voice through which God transmits His message where He chooses to send it. Those around you must see the atmosphere of the kingdom in your life; joy and grace are there because you represent the King. For many people, your life will be the only gospel that they will read in living color.

The possessed man in Gadara was the terror of that region because he was under the control of malicious forces. Once Jesus met him and freed him, the man prayed the Redeemer to allow him to accompany Him. However, Jesus told him to stay in that area to tell the people about what had happened to him. The man from Gerasa became Jesus's ambassador in that land and spoke to the people about the deliverance he had been granted.

Each one of us is a bright star in the spiritual and moral darkness of this world that leads and directs those around toward the Sun of Righteousness—Jesus.

Before going out the door, remember you are Jesus's ambassador in this world; you can speak to people about the land beyond. Live and act like you are empowered by heaven. Represent the One who gave you this wonderful position and ministry with honor.

I have chosen you to be a vessel of honor for My kingdom. I want you to bring the heavenly atmosphere that you have experienced in My presence into the world. I have made you My representative. People will look at you and see my grace. Speak to those around you using the wonderful words of My love and forgiveness. Step through the world on this day as a start that lights up the darkness that is around you.

The man from whom the demons had gone out begged to go with him, but Jesus sent him away, saying, "Return home and tell how much God has done for you."
So the man went away and told all over town how much Jesus had done for him. – Luke 8:38-39

All this is from God, who reconciled us to himself through Christ and gave us the ministry of reconciliation: that God was reconciling the world to himself in Christ, not counting people's sins against them. And he has committed to us the message of reconciliation.
– 2 Corinthians 5:18-19

Those who are wise will shine like the brightness of the heavens, and those who lead many to righteousness, like the stars for ever and ever. – Daniel 12:3

90

PROVOCATIONS

This made Saul very angry. "What's this?" he said. "They credit David with ten thousands and me with only thousands. Next they'll be making him their king!" But Saul had a spear in his hand, and he suddenly hurled it at David, intending to pin him to the wall. But David escaped him twice. – 1 Samuel 18:8, 10-11 (NLT)

As you meet various people along your path, some will provoke you. However, you must not respond to every provocation or engage in every battle that looms on the horizon. Choose your battles wisely because they will consume your energy and time, and some will even distance you from the Lord's plan.

The engine of envy started working in King Saul's heart at full speed. He wanted revenge on David because he had become the national hero the people praised in that time. He twice hurled his spear at David, trying to take his life, but David managed to dodge the threat both times.

Provocations are meant to test your character. What do you do when Saul's spear falls at your feet? What do you do when you have the chance to throw the spear back and stab the "Saul" in your life? If David had picked up the spear and hurled it toward Saul, he would have jeopardized his future and the divine plan for him to become king at the proper time. The mistake would have disqualified him.

In your life, you will notice that you will be able to bring justice to certain provocations, but do not forget that in God's school, He wants to prepare you for the plan He has for your life.

Before becoming king, David had to go through the school of provocations and learn not to respond but to be self-restrained. In the same way, you will also have to go through the school of provocations and learn self-restraint. When you have Saul's spear in your hands and have the ability to hurt it back to get even, remember that you must not respond to all provocations. Remember that Saul was led by an evil spirit and the provocation he launched at David was meant to disqualify him in the eyes of those who praised him in the "hit song" of the time. Do not respond to just any provocation; revenge belongs to the LORD. After Saul launched his spear a second time, David no longer returned to the palace to play the harp; he ran fearing for his life. "Saul's spear" will likely be directed at you multiple times. Be wise and stop going to those places.

The position and the miraculous plan for your life come together with provocations and with the need to respect the principles of the Scripture.

I will allow you to endure some provocations to reveal your character. Do not let others' negative attitudes influence you. I have plans for your life that will amaze you, but I am interested in building your character. In order to fulfill My plans, you will have to work with Me on your character. Accept the chisel of trials carving you into an exquisite instrument. I love you, and I will advise you what to do when Saul's spear is launched at you. Stay connected with Me, and peace will reign in your heart.

A man without self-control is like a city broken into and left without walls. – Proverbs 25:28 (ESV)

Know this, my beloved brothers: let every person be quick to hear, slow to speak, slow to anger; for the anger of man does not produce the righteousness of God.
– James 1:20 (ESV)

He who is slow to anger is better than a warrior, and he who controls his temper is greater than one who captures a city.
– Proverbs 16:32 (BSB)

91

Help Is on the Way

For I am the LORD your God who takes hold of your right hand and says to you, Do not fear; I will help you.
– Isaiah 41:13

Many reasons can steal your calm and peace, but if you allow the Lord's promises to flood your mind and the fibers of your life, they will chase away worry and sorrow.

All around you, people will rely on material possessions, on influential relationships and on extraordinary abilities. However, these impressive proficiencies and capabilities are merely illusions that fall apart in life's bitter storms. *"Some trust in chariots and some in horses, but we trust in the name of the LORD our God. They are brought to their knees and fall, but we rise up and stand firm."*

Moses, together with the Hebrew people who had left behind the slavery of Egypt, faced the Red Sea, which was impossible to cross. Behind them, Pharaoh's armies followed to recapture their former slaves and to return them to building the Egyptian cities and pyramids. On either side of them, high, unscalable cliffs kept them from fleeing. The people were caught between a rock and a hard place, between death by drowning or by Pharaoh's drawn sword. In that impossibility, no amount of gold, none of their relationships, and certainly not their impressive abilities could help them. God performed a miracle through Moses; He parted the Red Sea and the freed slaves crossed on dry land and were saved.

This familiar image reminds you that when you are caught between a rock and a hard place of life's nefarious circumstances, God has supernatural solutions to save you. He is the same unchanged God who is filled with kindness and ready to intervene and support you. Yes, He has unimaginable means to help you. Trust in the Lord and do not let worry come down like a thick fog to dominate your mind and point of view. Let the light of divine presence illuminate your darkness. Proclaim His help and His promises for your life.

The promises of His intervention hold great value when you find yourself in the maze of life's complications. Start collecting His promises in your heart now as they will help you or those around you when the clouds start to announce a storm on the horizon. Divine promises are like the lightning rod intercepting and canceling out the maliciousness of the Evil One's furious lightning.

Your trust in Me must manifest itself in the moments of sorrow and difficulty in your life. When the situation is complicated, do not allow yourself to be pressed down by nefarious circumstances or by people's attitudes, but speak to Me and let Me carry your burden. Pray and understand My solutions. Breathe the air of My presence when the fog of sorrow descends over your life. I will support you; I will create a path through the impossibility of the Red Sea that is before you, and I will lead you to the shore of blessings.

So do not fear, for I am with you; do not be dismayed,
for I am your God. I will strengthen you and help you; I
will uphold you with my righteous right hand.
– Isaiah 41:10

Moses answered the people, "Do not be afraid. Stand
firm and you will see the deliverance the LORD will
bring you today. The Egyptians you see today
you will never see again.
– Exodus 14:13

"Now then, stand still and see this great thing the LORD
is about to do before your eyes!
– 1 Samuel 12:16

92

REJOICE IN THIS DAY

The LORD has done it this very day; let us rejoice today and be glad. – Psalm 118:24

Before stepping out into this day, I want to remind you that God has placed various joys on your road. A contented heart and a state of expectation will help you gather up the joys of the day like a bouquet of flowers.

Perhaps you have difficulties that you need to face on the horizon or things that you have to accomplish. Do not forget that the Lord is your strength and your help. Set out on the road with the confidence that He is on your side wherever you step, and He will help you accomplish what is on your path. He will protect you on the paths that you walk along.

Start this day with a prayer of thanks, and make your lips sing a song of praise directed at the Lord. Thus, you will create an atmosphere where the Lord's presence emanates joy. Fight for a holy atmosphere, and the result will be fulfillment, joy and guidance. A joyful heart is the best weapon against the Evil One because the offers of sin will not be so tempting to a fulfilled and content heart. When your soul is filled with divine presence, the table full of shining apples from the Evil One will no longer be attractive. If you allow the tar of sin to mark your soul, you will feel the toxic smell and the burn it produces.

Fight in your heart so that the joy that His presence brings may animate your heart and your experience. Fill up on His presence. The Lord's joy is your courage.

Rejoice in this day that I have prepared for you. Stay in My presence to let your soul be filled with joy. When you accept My will, joy and fulfillment will pour into your soul at a much deeper level, like a full glass that is overflowing. If you do not accept My will, you will be tempted to taste the Evil One's promises, and they will bring you sorrow. I want you to let your soul fill upon My presence and for you to receive satisfaction at a spiritual level.

The LORD is my strength and my shield; my heart trusts in him, and he helps me. My heart leaps for joy, and with my song I praise him. – Psalm 28:7

May the God of hope fill you with all joy and peace as you trust in him, so that you may overflow with hope by the power of the Holy Spirit. – Romans 15:13

93

FRUITS

The LORD has done it this very day; let us rejoice today and be glad. – Psalm 118:24

You did not choose me, but I chose you and appointed you so that you might go and bear fruit - fruit that will last--and so that whatever you ask in my name the Father will give you. – John 15:16

Your life is a small branch that fulfills its purpose when it draws its sap from the vine. When you are constantly connected to life's Spring, meaning you are in a close relationship with Jesus, fruits will begin to show in your life. Bearing fruit is the sign that you are in connection with Jesus Christ.

Thinking that you can function based only on your resources is the Devil's trap. God's work is of a spiritual nature, and you need to feed from His presence. If your life's car goes on without fueling up from the divine tank, at some point you will become exhausted and make mistakes. Fuel up constantly from the Spring of Life in order to bear fruit that will bring praise to the Lord.

Your purpose is to be to His liking and to fulfill His will. When you try to please others, you will always live in a frustrating emotional rollercoaster with its ups and downs because man is ever-changing. Do not seek to please man for his acceptance; rather, seek to please God. The Lord's principles are clear in His Word, and His love for you does not change based on your accomplishments or your emotions. His love for you is a definite constant.

As you bear fruit for the Lord, you can manifest your love toward Him. The Lord loves you as you are.

The weeds that cause your life to be unfruitful and where you waste your energy elsewhere include the following:

- Worry, which consumes the energy that you should put into bearing fruit

- Accumulating as much wealth as you can, which is an illusion because you will not be able to take material things with you into the life beyond

- Coveting (evil desires) other things, which drown the Word, rendering it ineffective in bearing fruit

When you bear fruit for Me and My kingdom, you bring praise to Me. I rejoice and repay you through other things. So that you may grow and be strong, I will sometimes prune useless plants that stop your life from bearing fruit. Do not get upset when I cut certain things from your life because that is the only way you can become stronger and more fruitful. You are My beloved son and daughter.

That person is like a tree planted by streams of water, which yields its fruit in season and whose leaf does not wither—whatever they do prospers. – Psalm 1:3

Remain in me, as I also remain in you. No branch can bear fruit by itself; it must remain in the vine. Neither can you bear fruit unless you remain in me.
– John 15:4

94

THE CHANGE

Have I not commanded you? Be strong and courageous.
Do not be afraid; do not be discouraged, for the LORD
your God will be with you wherever you go." – Joshua 1:9

Often, in your mind, the thought of something new—a different life, a dream you would like to live—that you want to happen in your life will occur. Even as you wish for this new thing, the impossibility of fulfilling your dream also comes along on the horizon. Remember, God specializes in the impossible and with Him all things are possible. He can cause the deepest desires of your heart to come true—even when the mountains of impossibility stand before you.

Hannah greatly wished for children, but she was barren. Thousands of years ago in the Hebrew society, no medical solutions were available for her condition. Sorrow pressed down on her, and seemingly, her dream would never come true. However, after her prayers, God allowed a boy to be born who would bring her much joy and would become a spiritual pillar in those times. Because God specializes in the impossible, Samuel was the dream that was born.

The dreams that you weave in your imagination are also under God's eyes at the same time. He sees them and wants to show you His power by fulfilling them. Pray before Him, and

He will work at the right time. When it is God's will, the time will be established by Him. On the other hand, when these are also identical to your heart's plan, then nothing will be able to stop you from fulfilling the plan, dream, desire that is in your heart.

I am with you, and I will grant you victory. Do not allow fear to overtake you. Constantly proclaim My power, courage and support in your life. With My help, you will step forth into new territories and be surprised that my blessing will flow over your life. I see in your heart, and I know all of your desires. Pray for them the way Hannah prayed—with a heavy soul. Do not let sorrow consume you, but learn to release it before Me.

See, I am doing a new thing! Now it springs up; do you not perceive it? I am making a way in the wilderness and streams in the wasteland. – Isaiah 43:19

Be strong and courageous. Do not be afraid or terrified because of them, for the LORD *your God goes with you; he will never leave you nor forsake you.*
– Deuteronomy 31:6

95

REMEMBER

Let all that I am praise the LORD; may I never forget the good things he does for me. – Psalm 103:2 (NLT)

Man tends to consume the present with every fiber of his being and to launch himself into the future, forgetting what God has done for him. The memory of divine blessings that you have received and experienced are like vitamins for the soul and preserves the image of the One who gave them to you fresh in your mind.

Forgetfulness or spiritual amnesia is spread in the lives of the faithful. This forgetfulness can be treated through the prayer of thanks, which is a way to renew in your mind what the Lord has done for you.

The remainder of His divine blessings will help you in moments of fear and worry. When you are tempted to focus on yourself and on your limited resources to find solutions, remember that the Lord is on your side. The same way He has helped you and saved you in the past, He can repeat for you again. The experiences lived alongside Him will be a great support for future trials and challenges; they will help you to increase your faith.

Likewise, remembering what He has done for you helps you in moments of success when you will feel tempted to trust in your own powers; He will help you remember that He is the giver of blessings. From Him, through Him and for Him all things exist and continue to be. Remembering what the Lord did for you contains a great seed of blessings that can bear fruit in your life and in others' lives.

Review the gifts I have given you in your life. They will direct your attention to Me. You will notice that certain gifts you have received from Me were once a great joy for you. With the passage of time, you tend to forget or only vaguely remember these gifts. Find a way to record them and remember because they will help you in life's difficult moments. My marks in your life are of true value. Speaking about what I have given you and what I have done for you is a way to increase My fame on earth.

I will remember the deeds of the LORD; yes, I will remember your miracles of long ago. – Psalm 77:11

I will never forget your precepts, for by them you have preserved my life. – Psalm 119:93

96

DIFFERENT VALUE SYSTEMS

If a wise man has an argument with a fool, the fool only rages and laughs, and there is no quiet. – Proverbs 29:9 (ESV)

At times in life, you will see people who cannot reach a common denominator. They will contradict each other, even argue a point, and still not be able to reach an understanding. Reactions will either be laughter or crying. The main reason for this controversy is the difference in their values and principles, i.e., the wise man versus the madman, the lawless one versus the righteous one, the good versus the bad. Each of them possesses different values that lead them in life in making their decisions or acting in certain ways. When one person's values enter into conflict with another one's set of values or principles, the difference will be revealed. The peace will be disturbed.

Do not be surprised that in life you will not be able to be at peace with everyone. The reason why is simple: because of people's differing values. But as much as it depends on you, live in peace with all people and seek to follow the principles and values that you find in the Word of the Lord.

Prime Minister Haman, who is introduced in the book of Esther, wanted everyone to bow to him. Mordecai, whose principle was to bow only to the Lord and not to people, did not obey the minister's demand. The value systems of the two were in conflict, and Haman wanted to exact bitter revenge. God would later protect and promote Mordecai in a supernatural way.

As much as it depends on you, live in peace with all people. You will often have a heavy soul when you are unable to reach a common denominator with the other person. If you follow the Lord's principles, you will see that tension sometimes arises, but do not let the pressure get to you. If you do the Lord's will, you will certainly bother others who live based on another set of values.

Live according to the divine values presented in the holy Word and seek peace with all people, but do not forget that sometimes for you not to be upset will be impossible.

I am the One who wants to mold your values and form your principles according to My Word. Do not accept the Evil One's accusations in your life for the simple fact that someone close to you does not see matters as you do. Talk to Me and let Me influence your values so that you may lead a victorious life in all aspects. I will protect you and promote you, and I will turn things toward the better for you when you fulfill My will.

If it is possible, as far as it depends on you, live at peace with everyone. – Romans 12:18

The righteous despise the unjust; the wicked despise the godly. – Proverbs 29:27 (NLT)

97

THE PROMISE

You intended to harm me, but God intended it for good to accomplish what is now being done, the saving of many lives. – Genesis 50:20

The most unfair experiences you have endured are God's specialty. He will transform them into something good. This aspect of God, which may seem shocking and difficult to accept, is true. God does not allow hurts in your life just by chance. In His sovereignty, He knows how to turn negatives into something even better for you.

Joseph was envied, unjustly sold by his brothers, and ended up a slave. For thirteen years, his life worsened in Egypt's prison, and still, God turned around his situation. He lifted Joseph from his appalling situation and promoted him to the second most influential man on earth in his time. Incredible, but so true.

The story of Joseph's redemption brings rays of hope to the stories of our lives. We all have pains that sink us deeper into sorrows and questions, but Joseph has been whispering to us for thousands of years that God will change the situation to something even better that we cannot see or even imagine.

His brothers did him harm, but God changed the bad to good—with a purpose—to also save those who had harmed him.

After years, you will see that God turns your life's painful events into a story of redemption.

Thank the Lord in your prayers for the promise of redemption for your pains and sorrows, toward something even better for you.

I know that between the blows and the resulting tears, it is hard to trust in My plan. But I do not want you to worry your mind trying to understand how I will redeem the situation. I want you to trust in Me even when life makes no sense. I want you not to forget that I am in control even when your life's boat is being swallowed up by the waves. I will bring you to the waters of rest. Wait for Me to change things in your life and do not rush to take the problem into your own hands.

For I know the plans I have for you," declares the Lord, *"plans to prosper you and not to harm you, plans to give you hope and a future. – Jeremiah 29:11*

"Return home and tell how much God has done for you." So the man went away and told all over town how much Jesus had done for him. – Luke 8:39

98

GUIDING SIGNS

David asked him, "Who do you belong to? Where do you come from?" He said, "I am an Egyptian, the slave of an Amalekite. My master abandoned me when I became ill three days ago...David asked him, "Can you lead me down to this raiding party?" He answered, "Swear to me before God that you will not kill me or hand me over to my master, and I will take you down to them." – 1 Samuel 30:13, 15

Guiding signs are indicators on the road of life pointing us to fulfillment of divine plans, as well as answers to fervent prayers. Only a thirsty soul full of ardor and vigilance will notice the divine answers sprinkled on the paths traversed.

While David and his 600 brave soldiers were at war, an enemy army destroyed their city, taking their wives, children and belongings, leaving David and his army in the ruins of suffering. In their acute sorrow, the 600 brave men wanted to relieve their pain by taking revenge on David; however, he prayed to God before them for guidance and help to get back what they had lost.

Once they rose from the ruins of suffering to seek the marauding enemy, David saw a weak boy struggling between life and death. He fed him, and the boy rallied to tell him he was a slave of the marauders who had attacked his encampment and had abandoned him in that state. The boy was the indicator for the solution to their problem. The boy was the map to the enemy army. The 600 men could not see heaven's answer to David's prayers because their minds were darkened by revenge. David, who sought the guidance of heaven with ardor, found the divine sign to the situation.

Pray so that your heart's eyes may open, and you might understand more than what is apparent. Where many only see something normal, you may see divine signs. The sensitivity you will develop daily will help you to understand the map toward fulfilling your purpose.

I know this crowded and noisy world consumes your attention, but when you speak with Me, I will light up your mind and open your eyes to understand My plan. Make time to sit in solitude and prayer to listen to My whisper. You will see that, step by step, you will understand the signs that I place along your path in order to fulfill My plan for your life.

I will instruct you and teach you in the way you should go; I will counsel you with my loving eye on you.
– Psalm 32:8

The LORD will guide you always; he will satisfy your needs in a sun-scorched land and will strengthen your frame. You will be like a well-watered garden, like a spring whose waters never fail. – Isaiah 58:11

99

HUNGRY SOUL

You, God, are my God, earnestly I seek you; I thirst for you, my whole being longs for you, in a dry and parched land where there is no water. I will be fully satisfied as with the richest of foods; with singing lips my mouth will praise you. – Psalm 63:1, 5

Your soul thirsts and hungers for God, and these needs will only be satisfied when the soul finds its oasis at the Spring of Life and the Table of the Word. The soul yearns to be filled, and the promises at the world's table assure of satisfaction. Feeding your soul with material things and pleasures is a fleeting illusion, as God created the soul to be fueled with spiritual foods.

The parable of the rich man who invested and grew his stocks with material abundance told his soul: "Soul, you have many riches, eat, drink and rejoice." And the Lord told him: *"Fool, this very night your soul will be taken, and to whom will all these belong?"*

His material abundance was only an illusion to feed his soul with things that did not satisfy. His soul yearned for the breadcrumbs of divine presence. An abundance of material things merely point toward the blessings of the Creator and were not made to be consumed by the soul.

My friend, when you lose sight of eternity and eternal life, you begin to focus on this world. You soon embrace the illusion that you are not transient, and as you start to grab hold of this life with both hands, you realize later on that you are close to the end. Your soul is now starving, and you are a stranger to its Creator. Get close to your Creator today, as He awaits you with open arms and is ready to embrace you. Sit at His abundant table and let your soul be filled with His presence.

In my presence, there are joys and blessings, your soul will feel a great fulfillment and will be full when you sit in My presence. You will see people around you who have no time for Me and who race their life's car through life, but deep inside, they are thirsty for more. I fulfill the thirst of the soul. Speak to Me. I can bless you even in the areas where you are running and struggling. Am I not the Creator of the heavens and the earth?

Jesus replied, "I am the bread of life. Whoever comes to me will never be hungry again. Whoever believes in me will never be thirsty. – John 6:35 (NLT)

For he satisfies the thirsty and fills the hungry with good things. – Psalm 107:9 (NLT)

"Blessed are those who hunger and thirst for righteousness, for they shall be satisfied. – Matthew 5:6 (ESV)

100

RELIANCE ON THE LORD

For I am the LORD your God who takes hold of your right hand and says to you, Do not fear; I will help you.
– Isaiah 41:13

The Lord walks alongside you, holding your right hand and supporting you to help you step forth into the day ahead of you. When you live your life in reliance on the Lord, you are alert, you seek His guidance for the next step, and listen to Him. You will soon realize that when relying only on your wisdom, abilities, and resources will not be sufficient to get out of the complicated predicament. Divine grace and guidance will get you out of any maze of worry. The Lord sees well beyond what you see.

Many wish to live an independent life free of problems, but this is an illusion in a world that is fallen in sin. Jesus said: "In the world, you will have troubles, but take heart. I have overcome the world!" What you must seek is reliance on the Lord, the rope of hope, and divine guidance in the midst of the clouds gathering above you. In the midst of the storm, hold on to the rope of faith and hope with both hands.

Fight the temptation of thinking that you must know, understand, and control everything that goes on in your life. Trust in God when you do not understand. Do not doubt His kindness when life makes no sense but believe that challenges are the chisel that He uses to carve you into being more like Him.

You have often seen in your life how I have supported you through the challenges that you have experienced. I walk alongside, whether or not you are aware or do not feel me next to you. Though I am your God from afar, I am your God nearby. Reliance on visible things seems to give certainty, but reliance on the Creator of the universe, of all things seen and unseen, is the true certainty. I call you to a life of reliance on Me, and all other things in your life will change gradually.

Trust in the LORD with all your heart and lean not on your own understanding; in all your ways submit to him, and he will make your paths straight.
– Proverbs 3:5-6

I lift up my eyes to the mountains—where does my help come from? My help comes from the LORD, the Maker of heaven and earth. – Psalm 121:1-2

OTHER BOOKS
BY ADRIAN GHIDUC

ONE DAY YOU WILL UNDERSTAND
Trusting God When Life Doesn't Make Sense

FROM FAILURE TO VICTORY
The Unseen Plan of God